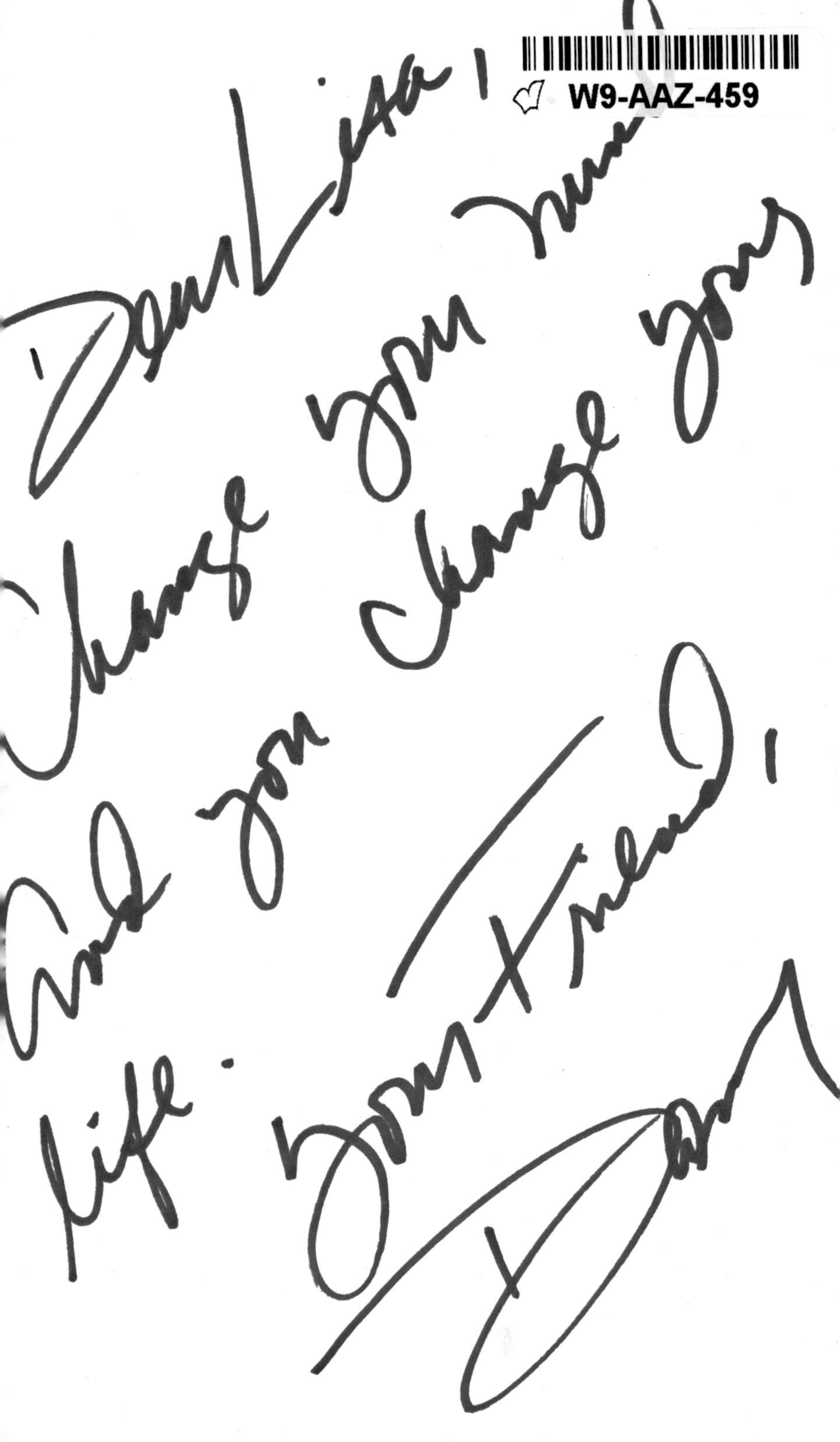

Dear Lisa,
Change your mind
And you change your
life.
Your friend,
[illegible]

Busting Your Rut

33 Practical Lessons to Alter Your Destiny, Transform Your Life and Free Your Spirit

Dr. Daniel T. Drubin
Master of Change

Published by 4th Dimension Management

To find out more about having Danny Drubin speak at your convention or work with your company, please contact:

4th Dimension Management Corporation
P.O. Box 27740
Las Vegas, NV 89126
877-540-4600

HYPERLINK "http://www.masterofchange.net" www.masterofchange.net
HYPERLINK "mailto:change@xmission.com" change@xmission.com

First edition

Cover Design: Lawton W. Howell, Sr.
Book Layout: Michelle VanGeest
Printed by Dickinson Press Inc.

Library of Congress Cataloging-in-Publication Data has been applied for.

ISBN 0-9708559-0-7

2 3 4 5 6 7 8 9 10

Printed in the United States

ACKNOWLEDGMENTS

I have been extremely fortunate in my life to be influenced by so many talented, caring, giving, loving family members and loyal friends. Without their support, confidence and guidance, *BUSTING YOUR RUT* would never have been written:

James E. Vassalotti I, Barbara Malkoff, Andrea & Les Hill, Deborah & Barry Drubin, Marlene & Saul Edelstein, Lawton W. Howell, Marsha & Richard Schoenfeld, Debra & Howard Lazar, Diane & Kenneth Kaplan, Leslie & Joseph Saxl, Ruth & Chuck Berg, Shelley & Jimmy Hoffman and Corree & Bill Grodnik. You inspire me.

To seven of the greatest nieces and nephews a person could ever hope for: Deb, L.Jeffrey, Robert, Jimbo, Bari, Victoria and Alexander. It is a pleasure experiencing life through your limitless eyes.

Alan Malkoff and Jerry Wortman, I miss you both.

The incredible members of CEO…you know who you are.

To all of you, thanks for riding life's roller coaster of change with me.

DEDICATION

This book is dedicated to my incredible wife Laura. Without question, you are the world's greatest friend and support system any person could ever hope for. Your strength of character and remarkable personality have opened my eyes to what is really important in life. For all that you have endured in the name of change and the strength you have displayed, you are indeed my life hero and a true Master of Change.

To my children, Peter and Jennifer, who continue to delight, challenge and inspire me, you have taught me how love can erase selfishness and how parenthood changes one's life for the better. Someday you will understand just how much having both of you in my life has made me a better person.

To my sister Cyndy, the best friend a brother could have. You are amazing.

To my mother, a woman who, in the face of so many changes beyond her control, created a real home for my sister Cyndy and me. You have taught me so much about life, integrity and giving to others.

And to my Dad, your spirit is and will always be alive within me. Your model of unqualified and unconditional love makes every day of my life better…your loss has changed me in more ways than I can imagine.

LOOKING BACK

I remember the day my Grandfather died. It feels like only yesterday, while in fact it was 50 years ago. I was five years old and lived on the third floor of a walk up apartment in the South Bronx, New York. The four of us lived in a $38 a month apartment in what could hardly be called the "garden spot" of New York. My grandparents lived in the adjoining building and the entire family had gathered to pay respects to my grandfather who was gravely ill. All of the adults were in the kitchen as the children played quietly nearby. Then, all of a sudden, there was a palpable change in the room. I had no idea what had taken place, but something had definitely changed. My parents and the other family members started rushing around, people began crying and I and the other children were quickly sent outside to play.

It was the first time that I realized a significant part of my life was never going to be exactly the same again. While I did not know how this change was going to impact my family and me, one thing was certain, someone that I loved very much was gone forever.

Obviously other changes had occurred earlier in my life, but to this day, this still remains my first recollection of major and dramatic change…the loss of a loved one.

Looking back on my life, I now realize that this was just the beginning of a myriad of changes that would and could occur on a daily basis. Nothing is ever the same from moment to moment, and one thing that I know for sure is that change, in all its various forms, is inevitable, ongoing, natural, normal, constant, stimulating, challenging, remarkable, controllable and uncontrollable. Change can make you happy and change can make you sad. You can be the victim of change or you can create changes in your life that enable you to become the master of your existence.

One thing is clear, change will continue to occur to you and around you, whether you like it or not. The only thing that you can ever hope to control is how effectively you manage the constantly changing events of your life.

This book was written for many reasons. It is inspired from my life experiences, a rich life that has been filled with incredible change, with more to come. This is a book of hope for those desperately trying to cope with the changes that life has thrown in their path and it is a step-by-step system for those wishing to use change to propel their life to greatness.

The message you are about to read can empower you to take charge of your life and help you steer a course through the many changes that life has in store for you. All of the stories are true and all of the experiences are shared in the hope that you will relate to and grow from these events.

GOING FORWARD

BUSTING YOUR RUT is not intended to be just another self-help book. Rather, it is broken into a series of practical, easy to understand lessons that are styled in such a way that you can use them as a reference guide whenever change appears...every moment of every day for the rest of your life!

For years people have asked me to share my secrets of personal and professional change. Actually, there are no secrets to change, just a series of practical lessons that anyone can follow. So after much thought, I decided that it was time to tell the story of how I have changed my life for the better.

To the extent that you apply these lessons, you can dramatically change your life and learn how to effectively manage the changes that you will encounter as you experience each day.

It is my hope that this book will serve you well when you are looking for inspiration, information, guidance and support.

BUSTING YOUR RUT begins NOW!

YOU CAN BREAK OLD AND LIMITING HABITS AND LIVE A MORE EXCITING LIFE.

Enjoy AND Evolve.

TABLE OF CONTENTS

This Book Has NO Traditional Table of Contents! Why should it? After all, this is a book about change and eliminating ***YOUR PERSONAL RUT.*** And in a world of ongoing change, nothing is sacred and nothing is safe. Not even a Table of Contents. Nothing will necessarily be the way you expect it to be…it's all about change. Only change is guaranteed. For most of us, life is a habit. We come to expect things to be as they have been in the past. We lull ourselves into a false sense of security by believing that everyone in our lives will always be there…that our relationships will continue to endure…that our jobs will be secure…and that what we have come to expect as the status quo will remain the same. In a world of constant and continuous change nothing can be taken for granted. Except, of course, change!

Get used to the idea that in a world of change, the only thing that you really can count on is your limitless ability to make the circumstances of your life better. Now is the time to accept total and complete responsibility for your life. After all, you do have unlimited opportunity swirling around you at all times. In a world of constant change, the only thing that really matters is how you face the changes and challenges of the future.

So while there is no traditional Table of Contents, I promise that this book is filled with lessons, insights, information and practical suggestions on how you can become a true Master of Change.

Oh, one more thing before we get started. For those who believe that just reading this book and the message it contains can change your life, don't waste your time and read any further. The only thing this book can do is act as a catalyst that motivates you to make decisions that will alter the rest of your life. After that, it's all up to you and for some of you that's the biggest change of all…taking total and complete responsibility of your life.

BUSTING YOUR RUT has been created to motivate you to dramatically transform your life and that transformation begins NOW!

CHANGE…IS TO:

Make different

Alter

Transform

Shift

Switch

Replace

Transfer

Substitute

Modify

Exchange

These are words to live by once you are committed to changing your life for the better.

FACTS ABOUT CHANGE

Change can be good.

Change can be bad.

Change can be both good and bad.

Change can have no effect on you at all.

Change is not always what it initially appears to be.

Change can be unexpected.

Change can occur right on schedule.

Change can be exhilarating.

Change can absolutely suck.

Change can influence your feelings and behavior.

Change can leave you helpless and numb.

Change can alter the rest of your life.

Change can have no long lasting impact whatsoever.

Change can be controlled.

Change can be totally beyond your control.

Change can happen rapidly.

Change can occur gradually.

Change can take place so insidiously that you don't even notice it at all.

Change can scare you.

Change creates change.

Change alters your priorities.

Change can inspire and uplift you.

Change can cause you to alter the direction of your life.

Change can increase your commitment to a life direction.

Change is continuous.

Change is inevitable…and because change is inevitable, your ability to effectively manage change is often more important than what happens to you.

That's why, more that anything else, becoming a Master of Change is not merely about what you want, as much as it is about your level of creativity and personal resourcefulness.

Show me an individual who is creative and resourceful enough to do whatever it takes to change who they are, and I will show you a person who can determine his or her own destiny.

CHANGE CANCELS SAMENESS.

LESSON 1

All Change Is About Loss And Gain

All change is about loss and gain, not necessarily your personal loss and gain, but global loss and gain. That means for every event that has occurred or will occur in your life, someone benefits and someone loses. Not just sometimes, but every time. If you take the time to look back at your life, I defy you to find any change in your life where loss and gain did not exist. This is important for you to remember, because with change comes balance, if not immediately, eventually. In fact, gain and loss can occur to the same person as a result of the same event.

You lose your job, someone else gains a job or the person in the unemployment office stays busy helping you and gets to keep his or hers. You are forced to relocate, you change where you live, give up a great residence, someone else gets a great residence and the person who owns the moving company gets a customer. You go to Las Vegas for vacation and lose some money and someone else wins some money, mostly the casino. Or, you win some money and perhaps you lose some valuable time that could have been spent with your family or friends. Hotels get built and the entire Las Vegas economy soars because of people willing to risk loss in an effort to gain. Your car battery dies, you lose time, convenience and money, the battery manufacturer and installer gain. And so it goes, one product becomes obsolete and you purchase another…loss and gain.

On a more personal level, the birth of a child can result in gain for you or others, as well as loss for you and others. The maternity store loses a customer, the baby store gains one. The obstetrician loses a patient, the pediatrician gains one. You gain joy and happiness and you get to spend money and invest in a college education. The loss and gain concept never ends. From birth to death there is loss and gain. You lose a loved one to death and the loss is obvious and so is the gain. The funeral home, florist, limousine company and cemetery gain. You may even gain by being in the deceased's will.

In good times and in bad times there is loss and gain.

In sickness and in health there is loss and gain.

In peace and in war there is loss and gain.

With every life experience there is loss and gain. Even when it's not at first obvious and even when you don't like it.

Once you are willing to accept the reality that all of life is about loss and gain, you then have the ability to alter the ways in which you view the changes that will occur to you during the rest of your life. You may even gain deeper insight and understanding into some of the events of your past.

There is a balance in the Universe. The idea that all change is about loss and gain empowers you to look for the positives in all events. And, while not all change may appear as a positive, you can seize each life shift as an opportunity for you to exercise your ability to grow and adapt.

If you assume the attitude that everything that happens to you in your life prepares you for the rest of your life, all change can be viewed as beneficial. Understanding the **Lesson of Loss and Gain** enables you to do a more efficient job of managing your life. What more could you possibly hope for?

How you view change is up to you.

Here's what you can do…

Refrain from judging change.

Remember that all change comes with balance.

The

end result of

change

is

freedom

from the way

things

had always been

done...

LESSON 2

Everyone Wants More Or Less Of Something

It never fails and I've seen and experienced it many times throughout my life and I know you have in yours. Just a little while after every aspect of your life appears to be in place and working perfectly, something captures your interest and that something becomes the catalyst of further change. It's all triggered by this little mechanism within us that constantly challenges us to do more and seek a better or different existence. Think about it and think about your life experiences. Total serenity in every area of your life never seems to be long lasting, to the point where some of us seem to have an insatiable desire for more. I call it the "I need new, more, better and different disease." Now don't get me wrong, this internal drive has a great deal to do with the desire to change for the better, and for most of us it's a positive and it's all part of life's great adventure. Whatever happened to contentment anyway?

What I am not suggesting here is that you embark on a series of changes just for the pure sake of change. Do not tear your life apart for the adventure of change. But rather take the time to sit down, either by yourself or with the people who matter the most in your life and construct a plan that includes change in a way that makes sense to all involved. Change must make sense in the grand scheme of your life's plan. Once you have your life's plan laid out, there are only two things you need to do:

1. Follow the plan.
2. Expect the plan to change.

One change leads to a never-ending series of changes that ultimately add up to your life.

As the famous Saturday Night Live character Roseanne Rosannadanna, played so brilliantly by the late Gilda Radner, used to say, "It's always something; if it's not one thing, it's another." True enough, it is always something. If you examine the changes that have occurred to this point in your life, that "always something" usually revolves around your constantly changing desires or the desires of the people in your life. And, while LESSON 1 deals with the reality of all change resulting in either loss or gain, this lesson is all about your aspirations and desires. For most of us, the desires we had as children are no longer important to us as adults. In fact, the desires we had yesterday may no longer be viewed as essential in our life today. For me, my favorite sports to watch and participate in used to be baseball, tennis, automobile racing and swimming. Now I hardly spend any time even keeping track of those sports and much prefer golf, skiing and basketball. Things change! By the way, I have always been a New York Giants Football fan. Some things never change! Same thing applies to hobbies. A few years back it was gardening and working on my car. Now, I would prefer to play my guitar and cook.

So if you have been paying attention to your life, it's pretty safe to assume that the desires you had in the past may have nothing to do with what is meaningful to you right now. And, while things in your life may be perfect for you this very moment, things are going to change. You can count on it!

Fact…everyone wants more or less of something!

No matter where you are in your personal or professional life, eventually you are going to want more of some things and less of others. Just remember that most of your desire and dissatisfaction is a healthy form of expression and comes from you taking inventory of your life and your desire to change.

Changing for the better begins with a decision.

Here's what you can do…

Be grateful for what you have.

Think big thoughts.

Extraordinary
people
do
ordinary things
in
extraordinary
ways...

LESSON 3

Change Perpetuates Change

I suppose this lesson could also be called the "Domino Effect of Change." You've seen it countless times. Push over one domino and it topples the series of dominoes lined up next to it. The dominoes continue to fall until you are out of dominoes, then you are done. Change is like that too. One life change triggers the next, then an entire series of changes keep on going until we run out of life…then you are done.

The sky is never the same from moment to moment. The same thing goes for the oceans and all living things. Changes keep on happening and one change perpetuates another. One oil spill in Alaska has a ripple effect that impacts an entire environment and economy. The seasons come and the seasons go and with each change comes a series of changes. Some of these changes are predictable and others a complete surprise. So if you are living, you are changing. Know for sure that one change never occurs without additional changes to follow. That is the way change happens, in a continuum.

As a matter of fact, it is almost impossible to change just one thing in your life and leave everything else alone. Change perpetuates more change and the changes continue indefinitely. Perhaps one of the clearest examples of this occurs in your home. One day you take a look around and decide that something needs to be replaced. It could be the carpeting, a bathroom fixture, the kitchen cabinets or just about anything. The more you think about changing one thing, the less appealing some of the old stuff around it becomes. Then you begin to construct a mental image of just how nice things would be if all of the old stuff were replaced with new stuff. It's a little game of change we play out in our mind.

When you stop and think about it, we really do possess a marvelous way of justifying our feelings and decisions and making everything okay in our minds. Interesting how when we really want something we can engage the creative and resourceful part of our brains and conceive a plan to make it happen. Then, we embark on whatever steps are necessary to create change. We get the estimates, figure out the financing and, as all these mental gymnastics are going on, we start looking around the areas we are about to change and begin to ask ourselves some questions. For instance, "How can I change the carpeting and leave the couch that way? How can I change the kitchen cabinets and leave the walls that color? If I change the bathroom fixtures, do I really want to live with that old tile?" The "Domino Effect of Change" can be seen in all areas of your life. From your wardrobe, where one new item can make the other clothes in your closet seem old and tired, to your occupation, where one change on your job sets off a series of changes.

You know exactly what I mean, because I guarantee that you have experienced this in some area of your life at least once. What's important to remember about change perpetuating change is that you will always be involved in a series of changes.

Change never occurs in a vacuum. Change perpetuates change...every time! One change leads to another in a never-ending series of changes and this pattern continues throughout our lives.

Here is why this lesson is so important for you to remember whenever change occurs. Every time a change occurs or is about to occur, create a plan and work it. Armed with the knowledge that other changes are likely to take place, instead of being caught off guard, you can take affirmative action and construct a plan that is consistent with the outcome you ultimately desire.

One of the most powerful weapons you possess is your ability to manage changes that are somewhat predictable and the ability to stay light on your feet for other surprises that life throws in your path.

You can control the next change or the next change can control you...take charge.

Here's what you can do...

Always have a plan.

Consistently work in the direction of what you want.

It's always easier

to

assign the

condition

of your life

to

outside forces…

LESSON 4

There Is Always a Price to Pay

Because everyone wants more or less of something and because it seems that most people seem to want more of something rather than less, let's spend some time discussing the price to be paid. This lesson does not necessarily have anything to do with money or any other materialistic possessions. While most of us want more of one thing or another and we are ready, willing and able to list all of the things we want, we usually do not want to alter our behavior to get what we desire. Well, if you keep on doing what you have always done, you will keep on getting more of what you already have. Oh, except for perhaps a massive dose of frustration.

I believe that many of us have come to automatically expect a bigger and better life just for surviving another year on the planet. For those of you who fit into that category, sorry to disappoint you. More time on earth will not guarantee you anything, perhaps with the exception of wrinkles, although a good plastic surgeon can take care of that.

It's time to face reality and our reality is that...all change comes with a price.

For some of you this comes as no great surprise, because you have been paying the price for years. For others, not only is this shocking, it almost defies your sense of reason. You just want more and you do not want to change anything to get more. Truth be told, if you are somewhat less than thrilled with the condition of your life, it probably has a lot to do with your failure, inability or unwillingness to identify the price of change and pay it. It has nothing to do with your looks or education or parents or religion or anything else for that matter. And, while certain life circumstances can make attaining success more difficult for some than others, for everyone who uses a difficult past as an excuse for not succeeding, I will show you someone who has overcome those same circumstances. These people who have overcome and have gone on to a more fulfilling life were bold in their actions and decisive in their thoughts. They became Masters Of Change. They took a look at their lives and made a conscious decision to no longer be willing to settle for the status quo. Rather than accept the existing, they took brave steps and made bold changes.

Don't get me wrong here. I did not say that accomplishing change is necessarily comfortable, fast or easy. What I am saying is that your willingness and ability to change is the first step to improving every aspect of your life. For those of you who are clear that there is always a price to pay and the condition of your life is still not of your liking, now is the time to identify exactly what that price is. Only then can you pay it. Change comes with a cost. No matter what anyone tells you, a better life comes with a cost and that cost is change. Your responsibility is to determine the cost and pay it gladly. Do so and you WIN!

As a child, your parents paid for the cost of change. Shelter, food, clothing, education, relocation, vacation, gifts, etc. For the truly fortunate, you cruised through childhood with little thought as to how you were going to cope with tomorrow. For those less fortunate, you probably were keenly aware that a price was being paid for your existence and very often tomorrow could never be taken for granted. In either case, when it came to your day-to-day survival, someone else took care of that for you. As an adult, the burden of responsibility shifts to you. Well, at least, for most adults. Most of us know at least one person who has gone out of their way to avoid paying any price for their lives. The end result is often a life we wouldn't want to change places with.

But for the majority of us, we make a change and we pay the price and it doesn't necessarily stop there. If you are responsible for the lives of others, your decisions have a trickle down effect that impact everyone in your sphere of influence. In concept, you can make one change and you may wind up paying the price for the rest of the people you are responsible for. Masters of Change recognize that the higher your level of life responsibility, the more change impacts your life and those around you.

As you examine the things you would like to have in your life as you change, it's important to consider the cost of change and IF you are even willing to pay the price. For anything that you have already received and for all the things you will eventually receive, there has been or will be a price to pay. Your job is relatively simple. Identify that price and if you are really serious about having more, better and different things in your life, PAY IT!

Years ago, I heard a story of a gentleman who immigrated to the United States from Europe. When he arrived in New York, he was hungry, found a restaurant and sat down at a table. He waited for service quite a while, but no server came to help him as they had in the restaurants in Europe. Eventually another diner came to his aid and explained to him how things worked in this cafeteria-style restaurant. He explained that you took a tray and got on line and once on line you could take as much food as you wanted. He further explained that at the end of the line there was a cashier and that person would tell him exactly how much he had to pay. As the story goes, the gentleman eventually determined that the United States is very much like that cafeteria. You can have anything you want as long as you are willing to pay the price at the end of the line.

Well, what **DO** you want? What do you really want? What do you want with all of your heart? Finding the answers to these questions is the beginning of creating change. I have been coaching people on how to create and manage change for the past 30 years and experience has taught me that determining what you want is best done in writing. As the old adage goes, "If wishes were horses, beggars would ride." If wishing or wanting were all that was necessary to change a life, where would all the fun and challenge be? You would already have everything you want and then be faced with a rather boring existence. The fun is in the hunt. That's where all self-fulfillment exists.

There is a lot more commitment to change when you invest

the time to write things down. The system that seems to work best for most people is to break your life into five different categories.

These five categories: Personal, Family, Business, Future Projects and Financial. While some categories have some overlap, I think you will find that just about everything you want to create or change in your life will fit comfortably into one of these five areas.

Your Personal list should contain things you want to change about you, or things that you would like to experience in your life. Your Personal list may contain things you would like to change in your eating habits, your exercise regime, or your personal behavior. This is where you would handle personal growth changes that you want to make happen, such as increasing your level of tolerance, becoming more patient, being more action oriented, eliminating procrastination or becoming more confrontational. You can also include hobbies you would like to pursue or sports you would like to get involved in. Perhaps you would include some continuing education that you wished you had gotten around to earlier in your life or vacations to exotic places. This list is about you, your goals, desires, aspirations, expectations and personal ambitions. Go wild, think bold and remember that the only limitations you have exist in your imagination.

Your Family list can contain all of the things that concern the people in your life that matter most. You might include vacations, your dream home or a vacation home, creating a college fund for your children, which may also appear on your Financial list. How about the quality and quantity of time you spend with your loved ones? Your Family list can literally contain all of the things you would like to experience for the rest of your life. This is your opportunity to be a visionary and create your own future. Sure life will throw you some curveballs, but that's all part of the experience.

Your Business/Career/Work list should contain all your professional aspirations and desires, from getting that raise you feel you deserve to starting your own business. It can be about filling that position that is opening in your company or taking your company public. This is where you can create your plan to continually reinvent yourself as you embark on new personal and business challenges. In this day and age, it's a rare occurrence for an individual to go through life doing only one thing. Most people will have several careers during their work years, so what would you like to do?

So far, just some of the things I have done include: managing a chain of boutique clothing stores, being a practicing chiropractor for 17 years, becoming the president of a national professional management corporation, starting a marketing and motivation business for doctors, recording five cassette albums, writing published articles, traveling the country as a motivational speaker and working as the director of marketing for a major insurance administration company. I can hardly wait to see what changes the future is going to bring.

Your Future Projects list is sort of an overflow list. It's the place where anything that doesn't fit anywhere else winds up. But more than that, the Future Projects list should contain all of the things you want to accomplish during the rest of your life.

What would you like to be? Where would you like to go? What careers would you like to pursue? It has been said that very few people possess the ability to see or plan their lives very far in the future. Sure, most of us can tell you about what the next few days, weeks or months will be like, but how about years from now? How about from this very minute throughout the rest of your life? This is your opportunity to be a true visionary, so have some fun, engage your imagination and as always, think big. After all, **BIG THINKING IS FREE.** As long as you have the ability to think any thought, why not entertain thoughts that bring you closer to the greatness you desire?

Your Financial List is where all of your money matters are handled. This is the place where you should have your debt reduction plan. Talk about change, imagine your life if you had no debt? It's possible if you have a plan and I will share my debt reduction plan with you later in the book. Your debt reduction plan can be tied directly to your wealth accumulation plan, which must be designed to create financial freedom. Yes, it can happen to you once you have the plan. That will come later too! Your Financial List is about future earnings, retirement funding, putting money away for your children's education and all other money matters, including having a registered and recently updated Last Will and Testament and Trusts.

Once you have constructed your five lists, the next thing you have to do is create a plan that enables you to attain your goals. The key in this plan surrounds the word, "HOW." I have always taught people, "The WOW is in the HOW." If you really want to WOW your self and others, you have to have an answer to HOW!

The HOW is your plan of action on HOW you are going to get what you want. To create your plan of action, I strongly recommend that you reverse engineer what you want. This means that you always start with your end in mind and then systematically and incrementally work backwards until you attain your goal. Your willingness to invest the time to create these five lists and work your plan of action is the true price to pay in this lesson. For without these essentials, you will almost certainly remain where you are and never be able to change your life for the better.

If you really want a life that contains more, better and different, the price to pay is often a steep one. This lesson literally demands that you rearrange your priorities in such a way that the things on your lists become your personal catalysts of change. This is the gut check portion of the book. This is the place where you get to find out what you are made of. It's put up or shut up time. For those who are truly committed to finding the greatness that you desire and becoming a Master of Change…get to work. Remember, what you get out of this lesson will be in direct proportion to what you put in…get to work. NOW! RIGHT NOW! Do not read the next lesson, it can wait. What matters RIGHT NOW is that you get to work on your five lists and your plan of action. Have Fun.

Success is a NOW thing.

Here's what you can do…

Know what you want.

Know the price.

Pay it!

THINK ABOUT CHANGING…

Where you dine out

The way that you drive

Your work ethic

How you treat others

Your intolerances

Your biases

How you feel about yourself

Your hobbies

Your views about money

How you use your spare time

Where you vacation

Your attitude

The Only Thing That Keeps You Where You Are Is The Quality Of Your Decisions.

LESSON 5

You're in the Pain…Or You're in the Pain

When it comes to changing or growing either personally or professionally, "You're in the pain…or you're in the pain." This has been one of my favorite expressions and philosophies for years. Initially, most people do not understand either the philosophy or the expression, but once they do and they embrace the concept, it serves them remarkably well in their day-to-day activities and their decision-making.

Let's face it, life is difficult and very often life is far more than difficult, it's nearly impossible. The good news is that you can make some changes and dramatically alter the quality of your life. Look at it like this; if something, someone, or an aspect of your life frustrates you and your life is simply not working to your satisfaction, you have some decisions to make. I have always believed that the most powerful possession that any individual has is his or her ability to choose his or her thoughts. For the most part, the only thing that keeps us in our present situation is the quality of our decision-making.

So if you are dissatisfied with the quality of your life, this is what you need to consider. You can leave things exactly as they are and remain miserable OR you can get involved in change and get really miserable. Either way, staying the same or changing, you are going to be uncomfortable. So, as long as you are going to be miserable anyway, you may as well change your life for the better. After all, you already know what you have and if for whatever reason that's not working for you, perhaps it's time to experience what lies beyond the ordinary, the routine and the known.

Intentionally seeking the pain of change is not an easy decision to make and it's not supposed to be. However, anyone willing to look the fear of change in the eye can alter his or her life easily and often. It's a matter of being willing to pay the price that change brings with it. Change requires courage…change requires tenacity…change requires a great support system…but mostly change requires honesty. Your ability to take an honest look at your life and your life goals has a lot to do with your decision to make things better. Very often people have to grow really dissatisfied with the current state of their life before they are willing to get uncomfortable and take the steps necessary to change.

The bottom line for the majority of us is that when we are no longer willing to tolerate the present conditions of our lives…we change.

Not necessarily fast, easy or comfortable, but we do change.

When the pain of staying in a relationship that isn't working becomes so painful that you are no longer willing to tolerate it, you will get into the pain of fixing it or changing it. Either way, you are going to be in the pain.

When you are no longer willing to work for what they are paying you, you will ask for a raise or quit. Either way, staying on the job or getting a raise or quitting, you are going to be in the pain.

When the pain of looking at your body in its present condition is no longer tolerable to you, you will begin a program of exercise and diet. Either way, staying the same and not liking it or getting into shape, you are going to be in the pain of change.

You name it. Whether it's a decision to continue smoking cigarettes and living with the consequences or the pain of quitting, you have a painful decision to make. If alcohol or drug abuse is an issue, or any other form of self-defeating behavior impacts your life, you always have those two choices. You can keep it the same and not like it or you can get about the business of change. Either way, you are going to be in the pain. You see, you are in the pain…or, you are in the pain. The choice is always yours. Keep it the same and settle or change. You get to choose.

My suggestion would be for you to take a real good look at your life and get in touch with your level of happiness. If you consider your present state a pleasant, fulfilling and satisfying one, rather than a painful one, you always have the option of keeping things exactly as they are. Of course, although things are going smoothly for you, you still have the ability to strive for best.

Life is an adventure. It's an adventure in which the clock is always ticking. So challenge yourself to get into the pain of change, just for the sheer joy of finding out what you are truly made of.

The pain of change often leads to pleasure. Find the pain.

Here's what you can do…

Strive for personal growth in all you do.

Be willing to get uncomfortable.

You are only
limited
by your
beliefs
and
many of your
beliefs
are not true!

LESSON 6

Decisions Determine Destiny

Three key ingredients largely determine your destiny:

- Your level of awareness.
- Your beliefs.
- Your commitment.

This lesson asks you to examine your personal awareness of the things around you, as you increase your beliefs about deserving a better life and becoming more committed to making change happen. It has been said that ***decisiveness*** is one of the key ingredients in all successful people. I believe this with all my heart and know this to be so. Nothing will change your life faster than the quantity and quality of your decisions. Change invariably follows decisions, so becoming more decisive goes a long way to improving your life. Each of us makes decisions every day. In fact, our entire day is filled with decisions from the moment we awake until we go to sleep. What to wear? What to eat? Dine in or eat out? What route should we take to work? Wash the car? What should the children wear? An entire day filled with never ending array decisions, one right after the next, up to and including when we should go to sleep. Some of the decisions we make come rather easily, automatically and require little or no thought. Some of our decisions are more difficult with huge consequences and demand great deliberation. Some people enjoy decision-making for the control it provides them, while others avoid decision-making at all costs because of the responsibility it brings and will often procrastinate rather than decide.

It appears that everyone's level of decision-making ability is different and our decision-making skills constantly change throughout our lives as we willingly accept more responsibility or choose to avoid responsibility. One day we make decisions for our children, the next day our children may be making decisions for us. One day we are taking orders from the boss, and someday we may be the boss issuing the orders. The role of the decision-maker is constantly changing and will continue to change throughout your life. As a child my mother used to make all of the financial decisions for our family, but things have changed. Today, with my mother's blessing, my sister and I manage her finances and assist her with other life and health decisions.

For each of us, every decision we make, whether it is for ourselves or for someone else, has a consequence and each consequence creates change. When my parents decided to change their lives and divorce, that decision had consequences and the result of that decision still impacts me to this day. You can pay your taxes or not pay your taxes; it's your decision and all of your decisions have consequences. Basically, you can do whatever you want, as long as you realize that everything you do has a consequence and you are willing to take responsibility for your decisions.

Of course there are those of us who avoid making decisions at all cost. I suppose, deciding not to decide is a decision. We either prefer to stay stuck where we are, either permanently or temporarily, or we wait for others to make our decisions for us. Given these two choices, I suggest that you take the offensive and make your own decisions rather than surrender the responsibility to someone else, especially if you are committed to changing your life. The moment you give up your decision making to someone else, you are literally handing another person license to determine your destiny. And for some, depending on your situation in life, this may not be a terrible thing. On the other hand, the moment you accept the responsibility of making your own decisions, you take control of your destiny. Taking control of your life is a powerful decision, a decision that can be both frightening and invigorating.

I have always believed that most people are compensated in life based on how much responsibility they are willing to accept. This goes to the very heart of being willing to make decisions and accept the responsibility of the changes that result from those decisions. And while there may be a few glaring exceptions to the belief that most people are rewarded based on their willingness to accept responsibility such as teachers, police officers and firefighters to name just a few, the more responsibility a person accepts the more he or she can change his or her life and the lives of the people who he or she come into contact with.

In order to accept more responsibility you have to be willing to live with the consequences of your decisions. This is where becoming a true Master of Change comes into play. Your ability to adapt to change is essential if you want to accomplish great things in your life. The goal here is to become incredibly flexible. The understanding that your decisions have consequences and the results of those consequences can alter the rest of your life is a powerful mental tool.

This is the time to begin making some bold decisions. Then be prepared to accept the responsibility that comes with those decisions and make the necessary changes as you advance in the direction of a more fulfilling life. I call this 3D Living. Decisions Determine Destiny.

Make some life changing decisions today AND stick to them.

Here's what you can do…

Make daily decisions that move you closer to your dreams.

Be fearless in your decision-making.

The more responsibility you accept the easier it is to change...

LESSON 7

Excuses or Excellence

Because your decisions create change, as you change you do have some decisions to make. In Lesson 6, we discussed how the quality and quantity of your decisions determine the quality and quantity of your experiences. Well, this is where we discuss the quality of your decisions. I call this lesson Excuses or Excellence, because when I speak to people about the quality of their lives and the decisions that created their present set of circumstances, one of two conditions generally exists. Either their lives are excellent, or they have some terrific excuses as to why things are the same or just plain awful. I continually find myself wondering how some people can be no better off than they were before they decided to change. I mean, how can a person intentionally go through what literally seems to be tons of changes and not dramatically improve his or her life for the better?

While it appears to be almost impossible, it happens to people all of the time. It's not that people don't want to change for the better or are not willing to change; it's only that most people are willing to settle for less than what they really want. And because we are often so willing to settle and still need to feel good about ourselves, we go through the motions of change and wind up pretty much in the same place. Then when someone asks us, or we ask ourselves about the condition of our life, we can justify remaining the same by telling others that we tried. Trying and staying the same has a great deal to do with the lack of willingness to get into the pain of change and plain old fear. Most true meaningful and long lasting change never occurs because we allow fear to control our performance. I call trying and staying the same The Martyr Syndrome. In The Martyr Syndrome you do just enough to make yourself feel better about your efforts but your life essentially remains the same because you stop short of true change.

Let's face it. Life's bottom line is about results, not effort. In most instances, nobody cares how hard you tried, the only thing that matters is results. People are interested in accomplishments not intentions. In your own life, you get to measure yourself based on what you have done, not your desires. Yet everyone that I have ever met that was unhappy with the quality of their life had the ability to rationalize and justify their circumstances. Every excuse for mediocrity made perfect sense, every reason for failure was logical. I have seen people in restaurants justify poor service or bad food. I have seen hotels justify lack of services in the name of great excuses. It seems that every time something is not as good as it was supposed to be, people have really great reasons that they believe can explain it away. Nobody wants excuses…everyone wants excellence.

In the end, it's all about excellence. Excellence attracts attention. You don't need a definition of excellence; you know it when you see it. In all areas of life, excellence is always obvious. In sports, in food, in personal service, in business and every other area of life, excellence is easy to spot. Perhaps this is because there is so much mediocrity that excellence stands out. Regardless of the reason, excellence should be what you strive for. Here's why. Anything less than excellence usually requires an explanation and the only thing people ever want is excellence, not excuses.

Excellence is not perfection. Yes, there is a fine line but there is a difference and so that there is no confusion, let me clarify. While perfection may be the best way something can be done, excellence may be the best way you are able to do it. Should you strive for perfection? Of course, and whenever possible, but in order to keep you sane, go for your personal best. When you achieve excellence, you will know it. You will feel it and the people around you will point it out. Remember, changing for the better and striving for excellence is a highly personal goal and everyone's interpretation of excellence is different. What matters most is that you are making positive changes and altering the direction of you life.

So strive for your personal best at everything that you do. Compete with yourself and become so fiercely competitive that you will drive yourself toward perfection. Then comfort yourself in knowing that all personal and professional growth comes from striving.

Changing to excellence is about improving the quality of your daily performance. If you are capable of doing more, or doing better, do it…why settle? Here's how to shift into excellence, just stop doing anything that isn't excellent. It's about as simple as that. You always know when you are settling for less than excellent, don't you? Excellence begins when you say so, it occurs the moment you are no longer willing to accept the ordinary.

Excellence is about your will, your attitude and your discipline. So, stop settling and go for excellence.

Here's what you can do…

Create higher standards for yourself.

Be honest about your efforts and performance.

Change effortlessly and often...
Even a tree gets rid of its leaves every year...

LESSON 8

Change Your Behavior And You Change Your Life

Almost all change comes from you changing your behavior. To a very great extent, past behavior shaped your past; therefore, your future behavior will go a long way in determining the rest of your life. So, if you are really serious about change, then you must consider the steps necessary to alter your future behavior. For most of us, our behavior is a habit. So much so that we often function on autopilot with very little conscious thought as to what we actually do. We just do. I guess one of the best examples is driving a car. When you were a new driver, you had to deliberately think about every little move you made. Everything you did, from starting the car, checking your mirrors, to steering and braking, all required thought. After a while, with experience, you can become so unconsciously competent that you just get into the car and the next thing you know you are at your destination, sometimes without knowing how you even got there. I have seen some people who have mastered this skill to the point where it becomes frightening to watch them behind the wheel. They can drive, drink coffee, speak on the phone, read the newspaper and put on make-up at the same time. Very scary. I think it's safe to say that, at that point, the behavior known as driving can become a habit.

Habits drive our lives and if you want to change your life you must be prepared to change your habits. Not necessarily all of your habits, but certainly the ones that do not support the personal growth you want. If you were totally clear about what you wanted, you would be able to ask yourself a very important question about your behavior. **"Does this behavior bring me closer to what I really want or not?"** If your answer is YES, keep on going and if your answer is NOT, change the behavior. For instance, if you desire to be healthier and live longer and you smoke two packs of cigarettes a day, never exercise and eat poorly, the next time you find yourself ready to light up ask yourself the big question, "Does this behavior bring me closer to what I really want or not?" Armed with the answer, you then have a decision to make. Remember, decisions determine your destiny. You could decide to maintain the same behavior and smoke the cigarettes and live or die with the consequences, or you can alter your behavior, quit smoking and reap the benefits. I never said changing your behavior was fast, easy or comfortable…just worthwhile.

So while your past behavior may have been predetermined by others or by yourself, your future behavior is of your choosing. Your ability to choose your attitude, actions and behavior is perhaps the most powerful possession you have; so don't take this power lightly. Choose wisely. In altering your behavior it's important to keep in mind that there is going to be a price to pay. Changing your behavior demands that you be willing to make some sacrifices. And as you would expect, the size of your sacrifice will very often parallel the size of your change. Big sacrifices lead to big changes and little sacrifices lead to more moderate change. Either way, the important thing is that you have made the decision to make the condition of your life better. What is important to remember is that you are changing and growing. Changing for the better is all about direction. As long as you consistently move in the right direction of your dreams, you will make your life better.

This would be a good time to take a personal inventory of your behaviors and habits. What needs to be changed and what can be left alone? What behaviors can be changed instantly and which behaviors need to change over time? Most important, keep asking yourself the big question…"Am I moving closer to what I want or not?" If you dedicate yourself to moving closer to your dreams each day, you can change your life and the lives of all around you.

Your past behavior determined who you are…your future behavior determines who you become.

Here's what you can do…

Be certain that your actions are consistent with your desires.

Explore new ways to conduct your daily activities.

You know you have really changed when your behavior changes…

LESSON 9

Change Is About Letting Go

This lesson is about your willingness to take a leap of faith. I'm not just speaking about changing behaviors or habits; I am talking about your courage, your resolve and your spirit. It's gut-check time. It's time to find out how much you really want to change. Now is the time when your actions have to match your words. This is where we separate the people who say they want change from the people who will ultimately become Masters of Change. This is where we separate the whiners from the winners. You get to choose.

Change is about letting go, and the person committed to change recognizes that to evolve from where you are to where you want to be, something has to change. As opposed to the person who says they want change and cling to the behaviors and habits that dominate their lives. One of my favorite expressions is, "The space between the trapezes is the exciting journey of life." I don't know who said it first, but the day I heard it, it had a profound impact on me. Perhaps it's because the visual is so vivid.

In order for the trapeze artist to get from one side to the other, he or she must be willing to let go of what he or she is clinging to in the hope that something better awaits him or her. Will the bar be there for him or her to catch, or will the other trapeze artist be there to catch him or her? And even if the bar is there, there is that moment in time when the artist is suspended in air just waiting. That's it in a nutshell. In order for you to change your life for the better you must be prepared to let go of the known and take the risk of grabbing onto something else. Think about it, that is the exciting journey of life. Exploring what exists beyond the known, beyond what you have come to expect, beyond the habit, beyond the predictable and beyond what is comfortable and safe.

After all, it's the things that you cling to in your life that have created the experience that you are having now. If you really want to change things, you have to let go of the known. I said this lesson is about taking a leap of faith and it is, because there is no guarantee that once you let go of what you have, you will wind up better off. I suppose a good question to ask yourself is, "How much do I really want to change my life?" Great question! How much safety do you want or need and how risk oriented are you? While safety and risk are highly personal issues, the reality is that if you are not content with your present state of affairs and if you are committed to change, you better be ready to let go of something.

It has always amazed me that so many people would rather stay in an unhappy relationship versus letting go of the known and exploring the possibilities. The fact is that some people would rather be miserable with the known than take a chance. ***Risk is***

good...not foolish risk, but measured risk. This is where the risk/reward ratio comes into play. The greater the risk you are willing to take, the more you increase your potential of a great reward. Life is energy. And the more energy you invest in seeking what lies beyond the known, the more rewarding your life will be.

So it all comes down to your ability to choose and your willingness to accept the responsibility for your decisions and actions. You can keep your life the same or change it. Stick with the known, or what I call your SOS (State Of Stuck) and settle, or let go and find out what adventures life holds in store for you. You get to choose and as you choose, remember your decisions determine your destiny. For everything you will ever want in your life, there is going to be a price to pay.

Let go of the known and pay the price of change.

Here's what you can do...

Place higher value on the benefits of changing.

Be prepared to let negative people leave your life.

IS IT TIME TO CHANGE…

Your physical appearance?

Your job or career?

Your relationships?

Your wardrobe?

Your television viewing habits?

Your exercise regimen?

Your parenting methods?

Your limiting beliefs?

Your diet?

Your bedtime?

The way you drive?

What side of the bed you sleep on?

If your life is boring, it's probably because the way you function each day is determined by the habits you have created. Bored? Burned out? Chances are there are some areas of your life, both personal and/or professional, that could use some changing. If you are uncertain about what to change, assume everything can be a little bit better than it is right now. If you are not sure about when you should begin changing, let me help you…

START CHANGING NOW.

You can only improve your life up to the size of your vision…

Expand
your vision
and
you expand
your
possibilities...

LESSON 10

Change Has Four Enemies

Change just seems to come easier to some than others. For many, the ability to change can be stimulating, pain free and effortless. For others, even the slightest amount of change can throw their lives into utter chaos and turmoil. By identifying and deciding to conquer the four enemies of change, you can turn chaos into order and change your ally.

Usually, when a person is stuck and unable to change, the cause is generally the result of one or more of four possible things:

Fear
Amiability
Complacency
Ego

Or what I refer to as **FACE.** Your ability to FACE what keeps you from changing is one of the most important steps in attaining maximum personal and professional growth. On the occasions in your life when you have avoided change, you can usually trace your being stuck to one or more than one of these very real emotions and personality traits.

Fear, Amiability, Complacency and Ego can prevent you from changing your life and realizing your potential. So unless you are prepared to meet each of these challenges head on, you are destined to remain in your present place. And if you are like most people, you will ultimately become extremely frustrated.

Fear is a great motivator. It can propel us forward or it can paralyze us. In the same situation, two people can act very differently. One person confronted with fear can face the fear and go on to become a hero while another person in the identical situation can run from fear and may be considered a coward. The difference is how each individual perceives the consequences of his or her actions. It comes down to a matter of value and everyone's values are different. If you have a fear of flying, when the value of getting somewhere in a hurry becomes important enough to you, you will just decide to overcome your fear. It has been said that the number one fear most people have is speaking in public. Create enough value for that person and they just might overcome that fear. Would you speak in public for one million dollars? Perhaps, it's a matter of what is valuable to you. Clinging to your fear of public speaking or getting the million bucks. Would you run into a burning building to save a piece of furniture? Well, not unless it was one very special piece of furniture. However, you just might run into that same burning building to save your child. Fear falls as value rises. The more you place value on something or someone, the more inclined you are to deal with your fears. I believe the number one reason people do not change is fear of rejection. The reason that you don't ask for a date with someone you admire is fear of rejection. The reason you do not ask for a pay increase or a better position within the company, even when you know you deserve it, is fear of rejection. We tend to place so much value on how another person might react to what we do; we just decide not to do it and stay where we are. How tragic. You see, it's not what you fear that holds you back, it's the value you place on getting the things you want. Call it leverage or call it values, either way, when you find out what is important to you, in any life situation, you will harness the resources to face your fears and conquer them.

Like so many other characteristics in life, amiability can work in your favor or against you. Sure it's nice to be nice, but not at the expense of being a human doormat. Now I'm not saying that there is anything wrong with being amiable. In fact there are times when being incredibly amiable can work to your advantage. However, there are times when being too amiable can get in the way of you getting what you want out of life. The overly amiable person will often settle rather than rock the boat. They often look for ways to please everyone else at the expense of their own happiness. They put themselves last and go along for the ride. If this sounds like you, is this really how you want to spend the rest of your life? Do you really want to be the end result of someone else's program of change or do you want to determine your own destiny? You get to choose. There are times when you are entitled to be selfish. To look out for # 1 and take control of your life. After all, you are the most important person in your life. Just because giving up some of your amiability is painful, uncomfortable and filled with guilt, does not mean it is not worthwhile. It's all about your confidence level, your self-image and how deserving and worthy you feel about yourself. The day you are willing to no longer live in someone else's dream and start living your own dream, you will give up some of your need to be liked and become the master of your own destiny.

While fear and amiability create one set of challenges, complacency is a challenge unto itself. Rather than confronting your reality, you convince yourself that everything in your life is just perfect and there is no need to change anything. So you remain the same. If this sounds a little too familiar, you may be kidding yourself, but you are not kidding me. I still have not met the person who has the perfect life. I have never met an individual who had it all and was willing to leave things exactly as they were. C'mon, be honest and look deep into your heart and soul. You know as well as I do that in some areas of your life you are settling. It's just easier staying the same than changing, so you avoid change. Then you concoct some of the finest reasons on earth to justify staying exactly where you are, in a zone of terminal comfort. You get into a world-class rut and spend the rest of your life there. There are lots of reasons why people grow complacent and most of those reasons are steeped in a person's self-image. The moment that you feel really good about who you are is the moment that your complacency will come to an end. It's all about your level of deservedness. When you believe that you deserve a better life you will get about the business of creating one.

Everyone has an ego. It's only when your ego gets in the way of change that it becomes a problem. Change almost never takes place in a vacuum. Change almost always has a catalyst. Very few people can make it through life without the encouragement and support of other people. If you are stuck and resist asking someone for help, chances are it's your ego that is holding you back. This may be the time to admit that you may not have all the answers. And maybe it's time that you sought the help of others. It doesn't make you any less of a person. On the contrary, when you put your ego aside and seek the wisdom of others, you grow as a person.

Only you know for certain if your ego is getting in the way of change. If it is, perhaps it's time that you embraced the pain of putting your ego in perspective and reach for the support of others. Not only will you gain the respect of others, you will change your life for the better.

Decide to conquer Fear, Amiability, Complacency and Ego.

Here's what you can do…

Stay focused on what you want.

Choose to win in the face of all odds and adversity.

The longer
you
remain the
same
the tougher
it is
to change...

LESSON 11

Conquer Your Fears

Of the four enemies of change, the one that seems to keep more people where they are is, without a doubt, fear. More people have been unable to change as a result of either real or imagined fear than anything else. I have never met a person who did not fear something or someone and I have never met a person who did not have some form of insecurity. Fear, whether it is actual or imagined, is a powerful emotion. Fears and phobias take on many forms and each person has different ways of dealing with their feelings or avoiding them. However, unless you are prepared to begin dealing with your feelings, you will most likely remain the same. Becoming a Master of Change demands that you address your fears and insecurities, at least the ones that you perceive are preventing you from reaching your life objectives.

Being afraid can stop personal change in its tracks. That is why there have been tons of books published in the name of how to deal with, manage, overcome, cope with and face fear. There are many extremely successful forms of treatment being used, including everything from psychiatry, psychology, hypnosis and meditation just to mention a few. However, for the purpose of this lesson I want to share some personal observations on how you can change the way your fears affect you.

Fear can take on many forms. While it would be impossible to cover all of the many aspects of fear, in order for you to change and grow, certain things do need to be addressed. Fact, most feelings of fear that a person experiences cannot be overcome with logic or statistics. Statistically we all know that flying is safe and driving without a seatbelt is not. Yet, despite all of the logic and statistics, some people will not fly and others will not buckle up. Laura and I have been driving together for over 20 years and despite the fact that I have never had an accident, whenever she is in the car she squirms at every move I make. I keep telling her to relax and she doesn't. The fact that we have never been involved in an accident has no effect on her or her fear. As the result of an auto accident she had years before we met, she is just not comfortable in a car unless she is driving. When in control she is fine, when someone else is behind the wheel she is not…all the logic in the world has had zero impact. Some fears can be overcome with control and other fears cannot. From a fear perspective, it seems the more controlling an individual the more they fear the control of others.

I have seen other fears overcome by passion and burning desire. As a young boy, my son Peter was an avid collector of sports memorabilia. Peter loved all sports, but baseball was his favorite and like most people enamored with a passion, the more autographs Peter could collect, the better. While Peter is extremely outgoing and confident now, at that point in his life he was very shy. What a conflict, wanting to collect autographs and too shy to ask. In those days we lived in New York and had numerous opportunities to attend local sporting events. Peter was a loyal New York Mets fan and we went to as many games as possible. As was our habit we would arrive at the ballpark extra early to watch the teams take batting practice. Once in the stadium, we would move down to lower field boxes and hug the rail in the hope of getting an autograph or having one of the players toss a practice ball into the stands. I remember one day in particular. We arrived at the ballpark and, as luck would have it, Kevin Mitchell, Peter's favorite player, was in the visiting team's line-up. The idea of getting a Kevin Mitchell autograph was incredibly exciting to Peter and as luck would have it, Kevin was giving autographs. What to do? At first Peter worked on me to call Kevin over, but I just wouldn't go for it. I told him that if he really wanted the autograph he had to first get Kevin's attention and then ask very politely. Peter's fear gripped him. You could see it and sense it. He was clearly torn about what to do. Pass on the opportunity and regret the decision later on or break through his fear and make something happen. After considerable deliberation, Peter transformed into a vocal and animated young man. At the top of his lungs he was yelling to get Kevin Mitchell's attention and Kevin responded. Not just with an autograph on a program, but with a baseball as well. Peter was a different person from that day forth. He learned two important lessons necessary for changing your life and getting what you want. Lesson one, if you don't ask you don't get. And lesson two, most of what you fear cannot hurt you. Peter's passion and burning desire enabled him to overcome his fears. You can do the same thing.

When we think about what we want our fears get in the way. This happens because we play the "What If" game. What if this or that happens? What if I don't try and people think I'm afraid or lazy? What if I try, fail and people laugh at me? What if I ask a question that others know the answer to and people think I'm dumb? What if I get sick? What if I take a risk and fail? Risk and failure are your friends. It's how you learn and grow. For some of us risk means using no sun block or running with scissors. The fact is, you can "What If" yourself to death and as long as you continue to do so, your fears will control your life. So to conquer your fears, follow these two rules.

Rule # 1-You are not allowed to play "What If!"

This is more important than you may imagine. You will be amazed at how many things will no longer hold you back the day you banish "What If" from your thinking. Yes, it takes discipline, yes it takes works and it's about as easy or difficult as you make it. You get to choose. Albert Einstein was quoted as saying, " Imagination is more important than knowledge." Well, for most of us, when it comes to our fears, it's because our imagination has run rampant, in spite of our logic or knowledge. Which is where the second rule of controlling your fear comes into play.

Rule # 2-Control your imagination and you control your fears.

All change in conquering your fears requires "up front confidence." The more you believe that you can and will overcome your fears, the closer you get to personal freedom, the freedom in knowing that you can change your life in any way that you can envision.

Every dream has a price and the price you may have to pay to live your dream is overcoming your fears. No more "What Ifs!"

Here's what you can do…

Make fear your friend and face it head on.

Believe that you can overcome any obstacle.

If change is not scary, it's not interesting...

LESSON 12

Change Requires Accountability

Significant change requires a very high level of commitment. You really have to want to change your life. And while many people desire change, they find permanent change a difficult thing to achieve. It seems that lots of people are capable of changing temporarily, but eventually we tend to shift back into old behaviors. So if it's permanent rather than temporary change you are looking for, you are probably going to need some help. Because we do so many things out of habit and because old habits die slowly, very often when we start making changes, eventually and for whatever reason, we lose sight of our goal and gradually revert back to doing things the same old way. After all, change is usually uncomfortable and for the majority, if you are uncomfortable long enough, you will seek comfort. It's why most diets don't work. You start out great, but after the discomfort of changing your eating habits you revert back to your old behavior and back comes all of the weight you lost. Comfort is the way you thought or acted before you made the decision to change. And while comfort can be your friend, when it comes to change, comfort is usually your biggest enemy. So how do you stay committed on your path of change? Easy, you find a Change Coach to keep you uncomfortable.

Some people love to exercise, not me. I don't even enjoy watching others exercise. I suppose that it's that whole endorphin thing. Frankly, I just don't get it. Yes, I know that exercise is good for me and I know all of the reasons why, so I do it, but that doesn't mean I have to like it. Despite all of the positive benefits, I just resent the entire routine. The changing of the clothes and putting on of cross-training shoes…yuck. Talk about change, how about the world of athletic shoes? They have a different type of athletic shoe for just about anything you want to do. When I was a kid, shoe selection was simple. I owned one pair of sneakers, usually Keds and whatever I did, my sneakers did, no special shoes. Oh well, between the weights and the treadmill, both of which I know that I need to do, I consume lots of time and, to make matters worse, get sweaty to boot. Eventually this routine gets to me and I quit. Sound familiar?

After going without exercise for a while and not liking the way I feel or what I see when I look in the mirror, I decide to begin exercising again. Apparently incapable of doing this on my own I decide to retain the services of a personal trainer. The trainer becomes my Change Coach. It's his job to hold me accountable and make me keep my appointments and torture and torment me until my body changes, which it eventually does…reluctantly. I can't actually believe that I pay for this. Once I'm back in shape and have committed the workout regimen to memory, I terminate the trainer, convincing myself that I am actually capable of keeping up the workouts without supervision. And for a few weeks I usually do a pretty good job. After a while, any excuse to shorten a workout or miss a workout seems valid and eventually I stop, only to go through this cycle over again in a few months. Having repeated this painful cycle more times than I am prepared to admit, my trainer is now part of my every day routine, forever!

Bottom-line…no accountability, no permanent change. There are some things that I can hold myself accountable for, but not exercise.

A Change Coach is someone you can count on to make your life miserable. It is the Change Coach's job to hold you accountable and make certain that you finish what you start. Your Change Coach can be a friend, family member, co-worker or a paid professional. In fact, almost anyone can qualify as a Change Coach as long as they are dedicated to supporting you in reaching your goals. If you ask someone to remind you to drink more water and they nag you all day long until you drink more water, that's a Change Coach. It's their responsibility to support you in becoming a better person, but to do so the Change Coach has to be very clear about what you want and often has to be just as committed to you changing as you are. A great Change Coach becomes a partner in your personal transformation. Therefore as you change for the better, you can celebrate your victories together. Celebrating victories reinforces your confidence and paves the way for future successes.

How about you? What do you really want to change and who is supporting you throughout the process? Are you really capable of making major change on your own or would you do better if you were held accountable? If you are truly committed to permanent and significant lifelong change, be prepared to get some help so you can be held accountable. Changing is more fun when you have a partner in the process. So whenever possible, find a coach and get into the discomfort of personal growth.

In an environment of zero accountability, it's difficult for most people to change permanently. Find a Change Coach.

Here's what you can do…

Seek the support of others.

Do what your coach tells you to do.

To transform who you are... you must transcend who you are!

LESSON 13

It's Not What You Know…It's What You Do

As a fifth grade student in the Jericho School system our son Peter was placed in the GEM Program. GEM was an acronym for the Gifted Education Module. Upon hearing that our child was considered gifted by someone besides us was both gratifying and somewhat mystifying. I mean, where could this miraculous gift have come from? Anyway, as the gloating parents of a gifted child, Laura and I were invited up to school one evening with the proud parents of the other gifted children to find out what was expected of them. By the way, all children, like all adults, are gifted at something! The challenge is bringing forth the gift.

The evening presentation began with the teacher giving the parents a series of brainteasers, which the children seemed to solve with ease, as their parents sat there confused, mesmerized and feeling a great deal less than gifted. Eventually we came to learn of something called Bloom's Taxonomy. For those of you who are teachers, by profession, you already know this to be the order in which critical thinking takes place. For the parents in the classroom that night, we were now totally lost. At first I thought we were going to discuss taxidermy, you know, stuffing dead animals. I soon came to learn that taxonomy is the order in which things occur and this is how our children would learn.

As I came to understand it, Bloom's Taxonomy has six components:

1. ***Knowledge***
2. ***Comprehension***
3. ***Application***
4. ***Analysis***
5. ***Synthesis***
6. ***Evaluation***

Each of these components is connected, but perhaps not the way you think. As a child, my family placed an exceptionally high value on education. I can still hear my parents' words ringing in my ears, "You are nothing without a college education." So, I went to college believing that a diploma would solve every life problem I would ever encounter, and then once armed with this education I would have all that I needed to enjoy all of the success that I wanted. I soon came to realize that there is a lot more to success than just a great education. As you know, education is important, but certainly not all that is necessary to get where most people want to be in life. Oh sure, you can point out the people who, without the benefit of a great formal education, went on to mind boggling achievement, but for most people, a well rounded education is just the beginning of getting what they want from life.

Until I experienced Bloom's Taxonomy, I never really understood how some people were able to dramatically change their lives while others remained mired in mediocrity. How could some people with great educations never seem to be able to attain success and how could others with little or no education reach greatness? Well, Bloom's Taxonomy put things into perspective for me. I figured that if the taxonomy worked in the area of education, the same six steps could be applied to how some people succeed while others remained stuck. This is what I came up with:

KNOWLEDGE

While knowledge is obviously important and essential for change and success, it is the lowest level of all personal growth. My parents were wrong and perhaps yours were too. It takes a whole lot more than an education to succeed in the world. Think about all of the people you know that possess enormous knowledge and go through life never seeming to enjoy the benefits of all of their learning. An individual armed exclusively with knowledge very often grows frustrated with his or her life situation. So, knowledge is important, but knowledge can be hired. There will always be some very intellectual people who will be happy to work for others, rather than control their own destiny.

COMPREHENSION

Comprehension is basically your ability to apply what you know in a meaningful fashion. Comprehension is your ability to understand and utilize what you have come to learn. If you can explain what you know, you comprehend. Who could possibly argue about the importance of comprehension when it comes to changing your life for the better? However, with only knowledge and comprehension working in your favor, exactly how far do you think you can go in the world? Probably not far enough, although a significant number of people are very happy at the levels of knowledge and comprehension and do not aspire for anything beyond these first two levels of change and success.

APPLICATION

Reaching the Application level provides greater potential for you to change and succeed. For those who invest the physical and mental energy to go beyond knowledge and comprehension, their ability to apply the information they have will allow them to take a quantum leap toward changing their life and reaching their goals. The Application level of change is where the rubber meets the road. This is where you find out if you just speak of change and personal growth, or are willing to make things happen. Application is your ability to take deliberate action on what you know and understand. It's essential to your personal achievement. More action-oriented individuals always have the best chance to alter their lives. Action-oriented people are just in the habit of doing more. The more you direct your activities toward becoming the person you want to be, the more you tip the odds of success in your favor.

To become a Master of Change, you must be committed to go beyond these first three steps. And while steps 1-3 can provide a great foundation for change and success, implementing steps 4,5, and 6 will help you achieve personal and professional change at the highest levels possible.

ANALYSIS

Analysis is the process of taking the first three steps in the taxonomy and assuming that things can be done better than the way they have always been done. Analysis is the literal process of taking things apart and examining them in a way that forces you to make decisions about a better way of doing things. McDonald's didn't invent the burger, they just took a look at the way things had always been done and through brilliant analysis conceived a better way. Disney didn't invent the amusement park or thrill rides; he analyzed the marketplace and created a unique way of entertaining people. Bill Gates didn't invent the computer; he just turned a machine into an art form. That's analysis.

To really get involved in the process of personal analysis, start with the supposition that every single aspect of your life can be better than it is right now. Then, systematically take your life apart and examine the components that make up who you are. The Analysis step of change can be time consuming, painful and always requires total honesty. Unless you are willing to come to grips with your life in its present state, you have little chance of making things better.

SYNTHESIS

If analysis is the process of taking things apart, then Synthesis is the process of putting things back together ***in a newer, different and better way.*** And there is always a better way. You might say that all creative genius is the combination of analysis and synthesis. You begin with the belief that things can be better. Then you analyze the situation, engage the creative side of your brain and figure out a way to make things better. People that consistently function in these two areas of change always come from the same assumption, "Good enough is never good enough and anyone or anything can always be made better."

EVALUATION

Evaluation is the highest level of all change and success. In this final step of the taxonomy you are challenged to accept responsibility for the other five steps. The highest level of change and success exists when you are willing to take responsibility for your life and the lives of those in your world. For the most part, people are not rewarded in life for what they know, but rather for how much responsibility they are prepared to take. The responsibility seekers change lives and change the world. They are responsibility magnets. Through careful evaluation they are willing to make the tough calls and accept all that comes with their decisions. At this ultimate level of change and success you control your own destiny and very often the destiny of others.

How does all this apply to you? Simple. If you had to place yourself in one of these six categories, where would you be? Regardless of where you are right now, what would it take for you to move to the next step? And if you really want to work your way to step six, how much responsibility are you willing to take…right now?

You change your life by advancing one step at a time.

Here's what you can do…

Willingly accept more responsibility.

Live with the outcomes of your decisions.

It doesn't make a difference who does it... it's how it's done!

LESSON 14

Find Your Passion

More personal and professional change has probably occurred in the name of passion than perhaps any other emotion. Passion has ignited wars, ruined marriages, inspired love, devastated families, created relationships, motivated artists, built business empires, won games and worked miracles. Show me a person who is passionate about something or someone and I will show you an individual that will not be denied.

Richard Flint is a valued friend and extremely talented motivational speaker. He has led an extremely interesting life, a life filled with massive change. One day I was sitting in Richard's audience when he said, "Passion and stamina are twins." When I heard that for the first time it just hit me between the eyes. **PASSION AND STAMINA ARE TWINS!** Show me a person who is truly passionate about changing and succeeding and I will show you a person who will continually work in the direction of what he or she desires. People with passion will always find the physical energy and mental resources to achieve great things. Fueled by passion, they will work tirelessly until they win.

Some Thoughts on Passion

- Finding your personal passion and stamina has everything to do with your ability to identify what is important to you.
- The things that you are passionate about will change throughout your life and that's natural and normal.
- Your passions ignite your spirit and enable you to call upon talents you may not even realize that you have.
- Sometimes controlling your feelings of passion is necessary.
- It's okay if other people are not as excited about your passion as you are.
- Passion can create pain as well as pleasure.
- Passion is a tool that can become your cornerstone of change.

So how do you find your passion? In most cases you don't have to find it, you already know what it is! It's those things you enjoy doing most that you do not have to do. The things you do outside of your work, your free time activities. I say outside of work because after a while most people are just not very passionate about what they do for a living. For those who find passion in their work, you are destined for greatness. But for most, it's the things they think about doing when they leave work that inspire their spirit and ignite their stamina.

Your persistence is fueled by your personal passion, and the more tangible the things you want, the more your passion comes into play. Your passion releases your brilliance. The area where your priorities lie is the place where your passion resides. A few years ago I attended a baseball dream week with the New York Mets. This had been a goal of mine for years. Being an avid sports fan and frustrated athlete, spending a week playing ball with Mets and other people just like me was the culmination of my dream. What a great experience, playing with the pros and even better being treated like a professional athlete. It's Day 1 and I am all decked out in my uniform, ready to take the field at the Mets official training complex in Port St. Lucie, Florida. This is just unbelievable, I'm on first base and as I am running to second, the shortstop fields a ground ball and, instead of throwing it to first, hits me in the right side of my head with the ball. I was knocked out and bleeding from my nose and mouth. The pain was excruciating and my head was swelling as I rolled in the dirt. The rest of the day was a blur. This was the first time I was in an ambulance, followed by three hours in the emergency room's radiology department. Diagnosis: 4 broken bones in my face. Swollen, black and blue, eye half closed, teeth loose and head pounding, it was recommended that I leave camp and go home. Confronted with my choices I made a decision. I did not come all this distance and pay all this money to give up on my dream. So, outfitted with a protective helmet and cleared by the surgeon, the next day I took the field and didn't miss a game. Your passion fuels your persistence and when you are passionate about something, you will find the stamina to accomplish great things. Yet, I know people who will miss a day of work because they have the sniffles…no passion.

As a family, we have always enjoyed fishing. Whenever we had the opportunity to do some fishing, the entire family was always very excited about the day. Today, my daughter Jennifer still loves to fish and whenever we go, Jen always manages to catch the most fish and usually the biggest fish. She just has a knack. Well, at age seventeen Jen places a lot of value on sleep and, given the opportunity, she would prefer to sleep as late as possible. But tell Jen that she has to be up at 5 A.M. to go fishing and she is the first one dressed and in the car. Why? She is passionate about fishing. It's that simple. I know people who cannot get out of bed to go to work, but they are up bright and early for a round of golf or a game of tennis. Why is it that people who will not bend over to pick up something on the floor at the office can spend their weekend bent over their garden planting flowers and picking weeds? It's all about passion. You will always find the stamina to do the things that are appealing to you.

Your mission is to identify the things that you are passionate about. Then, use that passion and stamina as a tool to make your life better. Remember, being passionate about something is a choice…you have the power and ability to be passionate about anything you want. It's just like flipping a switch and turning on the power. You get to choose.

Find your passion and you will find your stamina. Find your stamina and you can do anything.

Here's what you can do…

Create enthusiasm in all that you do.

Play full out.

Your aspirations will become your realizations when your purpose becomes your passion…

LESSON 15

Flexible is Durable

While change is a certainty, how you experience change and how change affects a person is highly individualized. A person's ability to manage change, whether self created or thrust upon them, is a very personalized thing and changes throughout a person's life. However, there is one thing that I can promise you, the more flexible you are, the more you can enjoy change and the less change will negatively impact your life.

The true Master of Change understands the concept of ***flexible is durable.*** Life is a marathon, not a sprint. If you want to win at the game of life, you'd better be flexible. Call it going with the flow or bending rather than breaking, the fact is that your ability to effectively adapt to change is all that matters. It has been said, "It does not matter what happens to you in life as much as how you handle it." Makes sense to me. Change happens and when it does you have two choices...react or respond. What's the difference? Simple. When you react you usually change out of impulse as opposed to responding, which typically comes as the result of careful thought and planning.

The goal is to manage change with planned responses whenever possible. Responding rather than reacting allows you to examine each situation and conceive the best plan of action to take. As always you have some choices to make. You can either move forward, backward or remain the same. Yes, one of the ways you can respond to change is by staying the same. On the other hand, most people think of change in terms of moving forward. However, the majority of change that I have experienced in my life and witnessed in others has come from moving backwards before you can go forward.

Let me explain. Let's say, for example, that your life has been filled with change and you have made the most of the opportunities that you have encountered. One day you take inventory of your life and realize that you are no longer content with your present situation. You begin to recognize that there may be something better in store for you, but in order for you to get to that better place you may have to first go backward before you can go forward. Almost anyone who has ever experienced a second or third career in his or her life knows exactly what I am speaking about. You deliberately leave what you have and start over at something new. When Michael Jordan, the world's greatest basketball player, wanted to pursue a career in baseball, he didn't start at the top in the major leagues, he started at the bottom. He had to go backward from where he was in order to build a new career. The fact that he did not do as well as a baseball player as a basketball player presented no problem. He just changed again and went on to win more championships with the Chicago Bulls. A true Master of Change, Jordan then decided to retire earlier than necessary to move forward in other areas of his life. You think it's easy for him because he has fame and wealth. I think he has fame and wealth because he is flexible and unafraid of life change. He is also remarkably talented and that never hurts. The world is filled with people who are willing to be flexible enough in their thoughts and actions in order to change their lives. And most of these Masters of Change are prepared to go backward before they can go forward.

Several years ago, I was faced with the opportunity to change or remain in a cycle of sameness that was dragging me down. I had built and run a number of successful businesses in New York but, despite the success and all that came with it, I wasn't having much fun. Sound familiar?

Just like you, I had some choices to make. Keep it the same and complain or get into the pain of change. I chose change. One day I came home from the office and announced that I wanted to sell our home and all of our belongings and start over somewhere else. As you might expect, Laura and the children looked at me as if I were nuts. They knew that I was dissatisfied with certain aspects of my life, but never did they imagine that I would actually do something about it. The clock of life is always ticking and I wanted a change, big change. I wanted to do all of the things that I had dreamt about while I could still do them. I wanted to go places that I had never been and embark on a new and exciting journey of life. I knew of so many people with the same thoughts, feelings and ideas, but all they did was complain and nothing changed. I was determined that this was not going to happen to me. Years earlier, as an avid skier, I had fallen in love with Park City, Utah. Quaint, intimate, friendly and environmentally magnificent, it was the exact opposite of where I lived. Talk about change, the prospect of moving from the high energy of New York to a little ski town in Utah was both stimulating and frightening. The more I entertained the idea, the more I was intrigued by the possibility of starting my life over again in a new place. So I began to run the idea past friends and family and their reaction was exactly what I expected it to be…zero enthusiasm followed by a deluge of questions. How could you leave New York? What about school for the kids? What about your business and ability to earn a living? What about leaving all of your friends and family? How can you just pick up and leave the only home you have ever had and change everything? These were great questions asked by wonderful and caring people who would gladly change their lives if they had the courage and the knowledge.

Most people have an enormous capacity to consciously or unconsciously convince themselves that they are stuck with the life they have, and then come up with some of the very best excuses I have ever heard to justify those decisions. For the Master of Change, it's not so much a question of how you can change your life, as much as a question of how you can continue to go through life and remain the same. Stagnant, bored and frustrated, most people just accept their lives instead of changing. These were the most common responses and, while many challenged my sanity and probably still do, my decision to change caused others to start looking at their lives in different terms. Did I mention that change is contagious? When you change, you become a role model and inspiration to others.

Well, the more I thought about what eventually became referred to as the Utah Project, the more I grew in touch with the reality of my life. I had never actually chosen to live in New York, it was chosen for me. This is where my grandparents landed when they emigrated from Europe to America in the early 1900's. This is where my parents were born and where they raised my sister and me. New York may have been a great idea for them decades ago; it just didn't make sense to me now. I eventually came to realize that most people didn't choose their life, others did that for them. Who chose the life you are living, you or someone else? Is the life you are living working for you or are you stuck and settling? Great questions. What are your answers?

Is where you are where you really want to be? If not, you have some choices to make. Perhaps your present condition is not of your choosing. Perhaps this is the life others planned for you and you are living out someone else's dreams instead of your own. Maybe where you live is where your grandparents or parents landed. Maybe going into the career you are in was someone else's idea, not yours. Only you know for sure, and believe me, deep down inside, you have these answers.

Perhaps if you were willing to start your life over and be more flexible, you would wake up each day more fulfilled and enjoy the challenges and changes of life once again. Starting over begins with a decision to change and the knowledge that you are going to have to be flexible. Starting over may mean that you have to go backward before you can go forward. For the Drubin family, each of us experienced the idea of life change differently. We also decided to be flexible and see what new adventures life held for us. Easy? Not necessarily! Uncomfortable? You bet! Worthwhile? Find out for yourself! Laura was both excited about the prospect of a new home, new business, new environment and new friends. At the same time, she was torn over leaving the place where she had grown up, the place where we had so many of our memories, where our children were born and raised and where our friends and family were. Peter had a totally different reaction and was immediately in love with the prospect of skiing every day, although he did have to start high school with kids he had never met before. As for Jennifer she had to leave her closest childhood friends, all 100 of them, and start over in a new place, all the while trying to figure out how she was going to survive without the local mall. Just like everyone else involved in change, I had my concerns and challenges. As stimulated as I was about this new life adventure, my emotions were divided. On one hand I knew that I had to be strong enough to support everyone else through the coming changes and flexible enough to deal with some very real emotions. On the other hand, I caught a terrible case of the "What ifs." What if we couldn't adapt to the change? What if the family hated the experience and me as a result? You can second guess yourself to death or be flexible and change. My bottom line…people are portable and if you are flexible, you can go anywhere and do anything. The only thing keeping you in your present situation is your thinking. Change your thoughts and you change your life.

Flexible is durable! People who roll with the punches are always better off because they get up one time more than they are knocked down. They have "bounce-back" ability. And while our move west was an enormous success, had it not worked, we would have solved the problem. How do I know? BECAUSE. Because flexible people always figure out a way to better manage their lives.

In baseball, if you want to get to second base you have to be willing to take your foot off first base. It's as simple as that…once again you get to choose. You can stay flexible and thrive or remain rigid and grow frustrated. You either bend or you break. You can never know for sure what the future holds, but if you are flexible, the future is yours to determine.

When it comes to change, flexible is durable…bend.

Here's what you can do…

Seek out the feedback of others.

Be open to better ways.

Your future
is yours
to determine...

LESSON 16

Complacency Kills Change

With the possible exception of outright fear, more desire to change has been killed by complacency than any other thing. So you think every area of your life is perfect? Your financial situation is ideal, your relationships are all working, your career is humming along perfectly and things couldn't be better. Who are you kidding? When you get right down to fact and reality, you know as well as I do that some of the things that you accept as perfect are far from it. I have never met a person who could not have an aspect of his or her life improved.

Having a life that is good should never prevent you from having a life that is better!

Complacency is a feeling. It is a state of mind well before it becomes a state of being. The problem with complacency is that it often leads to mental, physical and financial frustration. Rather than face the challenge of changing and improving our lives, we convince ourselves that everything is as good as it can be, even though we know, for sure, that we would like some things to be better. To make matters worse, we further convince ourselves that it's not a perfect world, which it isn't, so why even strive for better when things really are pretty good. I mean, it's not as if things are lousy. When things become really, really, really horrible, most people eventually opt for change. But, when things are pretty good, we choose comfort and tend to stay the same. Well, sameness can kill you. I am convinced that some people die prematurely because they have stopped striving to make their lives better and different. They die of boredom.

And in the face of things being pretty good you are once again confronted with the same two choices; keep things the same or make things better. As always, you get to choose. You can settle for what either is very good, or at least what appears to be very good, or you can go for what's best. Unfortunately, this is not always an easy choice, especially when most of the people in your life tend to want things exactly as they are. After all, there is a lot to be said for keeping things the same and not rocking the boat. You could probably make a very compelling argument that once you have found that comfortable groove in your life you should just leave well enough alone. Sure your job is not perfect, but why make trouble? Your family gets along well, at least most of the time, so why even attempt to address the problems and see if things can be improved? You have a nice home in a nice neighborhood, so why change it? The children are getting a pretty good education, so why find a better school district? You have a little savings for the future, why go for wealth?

It's your life; take a good look at it. Are you complacent? Are you going through the motions on a daily basis and settling for good instead of creating what you know can be better? If you are not certain of the answer, let me help you…you are. The problem with "good" is that it often masks your desire for "better." So you settle into a life that is comfortable, even though you realize that all personal and professional improvement comes from the discomfort of change. So why should you change? It all comes down to one word…**BECAUSE.**

BECAUSE is one of the best words ever created. BECAUSE is the word you should use to challenge yourself to achieve greater heights in your life. BECAUSE is your reason to grow beyond the comfort you are presently experiencing. BECAUSE is finding out about how good you can be and elevating your personal standards. The word BECAUSE can be all encompassing. That is why people use the word everyday to justify why things should or should not be done.

For years parents and bosses have used the word BECAUSE as their reason to get people to do things and will continue to do so. BECAUSE works! My mom used it with precision on my sister and me, and I have used it with my children with the same positive effect for exacting change. "Clean up your room." "Why?" "Because I said so!" End of discussion and end of complacency.

You want to know why you should kill complacency before it kills you…BECAUSE. Because it's better to change and grow than stay the same and settle. Because as wonderful as your life may be right now, today's good times will often lead you into a false sense of security and prevent you from having a better tomorrow. Your complacency will come to an end the moment you see yourself better off than you are right now. Never settle for good when you can experience better.

The number one WAY to change…LIFE REWARDS ACTION, NOT COMPLACENCY. Why? Just BECAUSE.

Here's what you can do…

Strive for personal greatness.

Elevate your standards.

What you focus on becomes your reality...

LESSON 17

You Get What You Expect

If you really want to change your life, change your expectations. The people I know that have made the most dramatic changes in their lives bring the expectation of a better life with them. They just anticipate that all change will be positive for them and for that reason alone they proceed fearlessly in the face of ongoing and sometimes uncertain change. Masters of Change understand that the quality of their life has a lot to do with the quality of their expectations. They know their expectations create their experiences and their experiences shape their life.

Is this an absolute rule? Of course not! You can go to a restaurant expecting a great meal and be served a lousy one. You can expect tomorrow to be a sunny day and it can rain. There are certain things beyond your control. On the other hand, there are a great many things that you can control, starting with your personal outlook. You can expect to enjoy your day and all of the changes that come with it. Then, by sheer will and determination you can make it a great day. It is within your personal power and your ability to control your outlook. Once you control your outlook, your experiences change. Expect to have fun at a party and you will. If you want to enjoy yourself, you control that experience. Does that mean making the best of bad situations at times? Definitely! Life is a teacher and within what sometimes appears to be an awful situation, there are often some very valuable lessons to be learned. It's a matter of attitude, expectation and perspective. Life events are neither positive nor negative, only teachers of lessons that we need to experience and learn.

You have the ability to change the way people and situations affect you.

Changing your life for the better requires a consistently great attitude and a high level of mental toughness. Your attitude creates your expectations and your expectations create your experiences. The more you can stay in control of your attitude, the more likely you are to make change work in your favor. When you remain mentally tough and control your attitude and expectations, instead of change being something that you fear, change becomes stimulating and exciting.

An important thing to remember is that you own your attitude. It's one of your personal possessions. It's part of your mental inventory; you can control it and you can use your attitude and expectations any way that you choose. While most understand the idea that it's your attitude to control, it amazes me how easily we surrender control of our attitude and expectations to other people and outside forces.

I suppose the classic example is what has happened to all of us at least once while driving our car. Cruising down the road, having the experience that you expected and completely immune to other drivers around you, some jerk cuts you off. On most days you just continue driving, giving little energy to what had just taken place. You expect some people to drive that way and you get what you expect. Then, of course, there is the day that for whatever reason you are unwilling to let the jerk get away with it. You feel it's your responsibility to at least let the other driver know how you feel, complete with hand gestures. So you decide to get even and the chase begins. Why people do this is intriguing to me, but it happens all the time. You see, I actually chased someone once and when I finally caught him, he was prepared to kill me. That was all the lesson that I needed.

Talk about change. Look at the changes that take place when an event like this occurs. You change your thinking, you change your driving style, you change your agenda, you change your emotions, you change your physiology and perhaps, even more frightening than anything else, you change your personality. You become a different person. Why? Simple! You lost control of your attitude and had a different experience than the one you had intended. To make matters worse, you not only lost control of your experience, you surrendered your life to a person who you don't know and with any luck at all, will never meet. You became the effect of somebody else's cause. You allowed another person to seize control of your day and alter your life. How does it feel? For most of us terrible, because when we calm down and think about what had just taken place we realize that our behavior was foolish and dangerous.

While the driving example is one of which I am sure you are familiar, all life is filled with situations and circumstances that either control us or we control. And it all begins with your attitude. Expect a great marriage and you are one step closer to enjoying the kind of relationship you expect. Expect a great career and you can count on attracting the opportunities and people into your life that will make a great career possible. Improving your life is all about your attitude of expectation. It's always your attitude of expectation that determines your experiences. In every area of life, you get what you expect. Have I mentioned that it's your attitude of expectation that determines the quality of your life?

Change your attitude and you change your life experience. Maintain the attitude that change is a good thing and you will get exactly what you expect. Maintain the attitude that change is your enemy and you get what you expect. Live with the attitude that you can attain all of your life goals and you will get what you expect. Live with the attitude that the world is against you, then change becomes a negative and you will get exactly what you expect. Approach each day with the thought that change is your friend and it will be. You will get what you expect. Make your attitude one of great persistence and eventually you will find the passion and stamina to achieve great things in your life. You get what you expect. And as long as you get what you expect, how about improving your expectations? Now that's a change for the better.

Maintain an attitude of great expectations and you will get exactly what you expect.

Here's what you can do…

Look for the good in others.

Find the upside of all life events.

Big
change
can come from
little
decisions…

LESSON 18

Raise Your Standards

As long as you are committed to change, why settle? Now is the time to look at the standards by which you live and take personal inventory. Are you settling? Well, if you are like the majority of people, you probably are! The good news is that it doesn't matter what you have experienced up to this point in your life, the only thing that counts is what you do next. While it's beyond your ability to alter the past, there is a great deal that you can do about your future.

Because all change begins with an idea, in order to change, you must be prepared to entertain all thoughts that cross your mind. In your mind, you have the limitless freedom to consider any idea that appeals to you, as long as you are free to think any thought you want, think bigger than you do right now. After all, it takes the same amount of energy to think a big thought as a small thought. So why limit what is possible for you to achieve? Dare to think grander thoughts than you ever have before and begin to imagine just how you can change your personal world for the better. Think about all of the big changes that you have overcome to this point in your life and use that positive feedback to enable you to shape your future.

BIG THINKING IS FREE...NO CHARGE FOR THINKING LARGE!

Once you have locked your mind onto what you want, the next thing you need to do is strive for excellence. Excellence attracts attention; therefore, you will win the admiration of other people. You always know excellence when you see it and it's easy to recognize things that are less than excellent. Well, just how good can you make your life? That's up to you! You can make little changes and change your life a little; you can make big and bold changes and change your life dramatically or you can remain exactly where you are. It's all up to you. I believe that you can only improve your life up to the standards that you have set for yourself or that you have allowed others to set for you. The higher your standards, the greater your potential for a better life.

Take control and determine your own standards for excellence.

Only you know for sure if your standards of excellence are high enough. For years, people have told me to set realistic goals. Then someone told me what the code word for realistic is...LOW! Realistic goals do not allow you to stretch and grow. By setting high standards for yourself, you will have a life filled with the challenges and rewards that come from giving your personal best. That's what you want isn't it? So where do you begin? With the very next thing that you decide to do. Raising your standards begins with a conscious decision to be better at each task you undertake, one task at a time.

As you approach each task or project, regardless of how large or small, ask yourself, "Am I settling? Is this the best that I can do? Am I holding back or giving all I've got? Am I settling for mediocrity or am I working consistently to achieve personal excellence?" If you answer honestly, and you may as well, you will find that in many instances you could have done better. The beginning of elevating your standards comes with the recognition that you could have done better. Once you are prepared to deal with that truth, the next question that needs to be answered is, "Why bother?" Why should you do your personal best when so many people are willing to accept less than the best? Simple. For the shear joy of finding out just how good you can be. And the only person who you have to please in this entire exercise is you. You raise your personal standards for the gratification of doing your personal best. Like most things, elevating your standards begins with the idea that you can do better and eventually becomes a personal challenge that is directed by your will and personal discipline.

Starting right now you can decide to do better at anything you undertake. Eventually, the habit of doing everything better will become the culture in which you live your life.

Have you ever wondered how whales are able to jump so high? The trainers continue to raise the standards for the whale until it is no longer able to propel itself any higher through the air. This is done by gradually altering the whale's behavior through a series of rewards for good behavior and no rewards for substandard behavior. When it comes to personal achievement, we are kind of like the whales. We either move toward rewards when it comes to our behavior or we shy away from penalties whenever we are threatened. Unlike the whale, most of us have no one raising the standards for us; we have to do that on our own, unless of course you have a Change Coach. While the whale can be motivated by a bucket of fish, your goal is to find out what makes you jump. Once you do, keep raising the bar until you have maximized your personal potential.

While in high school, my daughter Jennifer worked as a salesperson at the Sunglass Hut on Main Street in Park City, Utah. Whatever Jen does in life, she takes very seriously and she approached this job with the same zeal and energy that she approaches life. Like most businesses, Sunglass Hut has production goals with each store responsible for reaching or exceeding their sales numbers each day. On one particularly quiet day in the store, with few potential customers coming in and hardly any sales to show for her efforts, Jen decided to make some changes in the way business had been conducted. Rather than just sit around the store all day and wait for something to happen, she decided to go on the offensive and make something happen. This is what she did. Armed with a spray bottle of sunglass cleaner and a cleaning cloth, she stood outside the store offering to clean people's sunglasses for free. In only a few minutes her efforts attracted a long line of people wanting their glasses cleaned. As she cleaned people's glasses she began to describe some of the sunglasses in the store that they might want to look at. In no time at all the crowd had moved from the street into the store and Jen was showing and selling sunglasses at a record pace. Needless to say her bold actions resulted in exceeding the store's sales goals for the day. Like most people, Jen had some choices. She could sit around with an employee's attitude and just be happy to collect her hourly wage or she could elevate her standards, get creative and make some changes in the way business was conducted.

Each day you are faced with those same two choices: maintain the status quo, go through the motions, collect your wage and leave your standards exactly where they are OR raise your standards and aggressively change the way things are done. Elevating your standards is about achieving your personal best and playing full out in the game of life.

Elevate your standards and you elevate the quality of your life.

Here's what you can do…

Fully invest yourself in each thing you do.

Never settle for good when excellence can be achieved.

Either
you become
a master
of change
or
a slave to it...

LESSON 19

Rapid Change Requires Rapid Response

Once you make the commitment to change your life for the better, the next thing to consider is the speed of change. Change occurs the moment you are willing to accept all of the responsibility that change brings with it. However, the speed of change is different for everyone. With the clock of life always ticking and time our most precious commodity, the rapidity of change becomes a life asset. Let's face it, the faster you can make your life better, the better! After all, we are not growing a redwood tree and we don't have a zillion years to alter our lives, so get on with it.

In order for you to change rapidly, you must be prepared to mobilize all of your available resources. That means seeking the help of others whenever and wherever you can. Rapid change requires you to put your ego aside and find people who are willing to help you facilitate the change you desire. It also means that you must harness your mental and physical energy and create a workable plan that supports you in attaining your desired outcome. This plan needs to be incredibly precise and conceived in such detail that nothing is left to chance and the change you want to experience is virtually assured. And as a mindset you should be prepared to do whatever it takes to reach your goal. This demands that you become unwilling to accept NO as an answer. For the person committed to change, victory is all he or she will settle for, despite the setbacks he or she may experience along the way. The Master of Change understands that these obstacles are there to test his or her fortitude, strengthen his or her resolve and make him or her want to succeed even more.

Remember, you can either allow change to happen to you and deal with it to the best of your ability or you can create change, it's all up to you. You get to choose. If you choose to create change, a good place to start is by evaluating your present situation. Once you know exactly where you are and you know exactly what you want, you can conceive a plan that makes change happen for you. Just keep in mind that in order for you to make rapid changes, you have to be extremely responsive and massively action oriented. A strategy of well directed actions will usually get you the changes you want, especially if you have a team of supporters prepared to help you as your plan unfolds. Do you have a support team? Or, are you going it all alone? Perhaps it's time to start recruiting some people who want to help you improve your life. It's easier than you think. All you have to do is ASK!

My son Peter had already graduated from Park City High School and had been accepted to attend the University of Utah. Although still uncertain about the career he wanted to pursue, Peter seemed truly excited about going to the U of U. Needless to say we were thrilled with his choice, after all, we would have him close to home, which would account for minor change, rather than massive change. Just when we were looking at dormitories for him and getting ready for him to go, he had a sudden awakening. Something changed in Peter. Almost as if by magic he made a series of major decisions and in the span of one day he decided on his life's direction. Because one change always creates a ripple effect, as the result of Peter's change of mind, everything in my life began to change at a whirlwind pace. One afternoon Peter emerged from his bedroom and made the following announcement, "I have decided to major in business and finance and my personal interests would be best served by going to school in New York." Talk about change! It was all very exciting, pretty impressive and a little bit scary. In one day Peter decided on a life direction, but in order for us to support him in his goals, a great deal had to take place in a very short period of time. We had to find a college with a great business program and we did, Hofstra University. We had to get an application, fill it out; overnight it back and hope that the school had room for one very determined and very late applicant. So our team took immediate action. It took dozens of phone calls, Federal Express mailings, finding and forwarding transcripts, arranging finances and securing housing. Sound tough? Well, it was. But despite all of the challenges that the task demanded, within two weeks Peter had been accepted to the School of Business at Hofstra University. Pretty cool, huh? It just goes to show what can be accomplished when a team of people is willing to align behind a common objective. Had it not been for the massive action of our family and friends, Peter would not have been able to fulfill his dream.

You can control the speed of change…sometimes!

There was a time in my life when fast cars and automobile racing were all I thought about. I had always considered myself a pretty good driver and I was so filled with enthusiasm to race, I attended as many sports car races as possible. One weekend I was invited by a friend to attend an auto race at Bridgehampton Motor Speedway on Long Island. Being able to spend time in the pits with the drivers was really exciting and as the races began and I watched, I was literally captivated by the idea that I would like to try this. It seemed like the making of a dream come true. I made all the necessary preparations including taking my only car, a 1972 Datsun 240Z, and converting it into a fully prepared race car. Then I enlisted the support of one of the drivers I had met at the track and asked him if he would help me get my racing license. He said yes and I enrolled in racing school. It seemed fairly simple at first. All of the drivers met and discussed the upcoming events of the day including how to make it around the racecourse safely and quickly. This is the way the day was scheduled to work. First, the person who was helping you get your license would get behind the wheel of your car and you would strap into the passenger seat. Then, very slowly the instructor would drive around the track pointing out where the car should be at each turn. After doing this for a while, the instructor proceeded to drive around the track at race speed, as I hung on for dear life. This was as frightening an experience as I had ever had. Imagine yourself having no control over what was taking place, with someone else at the wheel of your only car. Well, we flew around the track for a while and eventually it was my turn to drive. And so, we switched places with me behind the wheel for the first time and the experienced race car driver in the passenger seat. If I was scared, he must have been terrified. My instructions were quite clear. Drive the course nice and slow to get the feel of the car and get used to the layout of the racecourse. Which is exactly what I did and I must admit, I was feeling pretty good about the entire experience. I was looking cool in my race suit and helmet and at the wheel of a great looking race car. Having accomplished my initial goal, it was now my turn to drive as fast as I could. So I picked up speed and put the car through its paces driving as fast as I could and faster than I had ever driven before. Just then something terrifying happened. The instructor in the passenger seat lifted up his left foot, moved it over the gearbox and smashed his foot down over my right foot, which drove the accelerator to the floor. Talk about change? I had just lost control of the speed of the car and, while I thought I was going fast before, the only thing I could do was hang on and steer faster. Eventually, when sheer terror subsided, I became used to the speed… only then did I really understand what it took to win a race. Later, after I regained my composure, I asked the instructor why he did what he did. This is what he said, "If you ever expect to win, you've got to go through life with your right foot down."

I never forgot those words and have used the concept of "Right foot down" to my advantage whenever I wanted to make dramatic and rapid change in my life. Hopefully, this story will remain fresh in your mind and the next time you are ready for change you will keep your "Right foot down" and accelerate the speed in which you make change happen.

As long as you are changing, change rapidly.

Here's what you can do…

Approach all you do with greater urgency.

Put your energy where it matters most.

Everyone's reasons for remaining the same are always perfect!

LESSON 20

Catch F.I.R.E.

You can fuel change through inspiration. People who are inspired to change feel a burning desire to make their lives better. This feeling courses through their minds and bodies as they diligently work to improve the quality of their lives. And, while inspiration cannot always be seen to the naked eye, the results of inspiration can be witnessed in the increased determination of a person intent on becoming a Master of Change.

Whether you are creating change, coping with change or managing change, the greater your personal energy is the more effective you can be. And the more you can focus your personal energy, the more inspiration you can direct toward the changes you want to make. Over the years, I have identified four key ingredients to change that have worked wonders for me and hopefully they will for you too. I use the acronym F.I.R.E. as my guide whenever I want to create change in any area of my life.

F - FOCUS
I - INTENSITY
R - RESOURCEFULNESS
E - ENTHUSIASM

Focus is your ability and willingness to clearly identify what needs to be done and then place all of your mental and physical energy into the project. The ability to direct all of your energy and attention on change is what enables you to change rapidly, efficiently and often. When you are truly focused, change becomes the central activity of your life, thus all of your concentration becomes directed to accomplishing whatever needs to be done. Being focused demands great discipline and is essential if you want to make changing for the better a life priority. Change then becomes the major precedent in your life, even at the expense of other people and events. You become unstoppable in your determination as all of your energy is directed toward personal improvement. You live to change and you love it. Like most personal disciplines, everyone's ability to focus on a particular situation is different. Some people are able to totally zone in on what needs to be done, others are only able to focus for short bursts of time, while yet others are seemingly unable to focus at all. I believe that a person's ability to focus consistently has more to do with their priorities than anything else. Show me an individual that is clear about his or her priorities and I will show you a person who is capable of great focus. Bottom line…the more you make change a pressing priority in your life, the greater your will power becomes, subsequently focusing becomes easy as well as fun. There is a lot to be said about only having to deal with one thing, your burning desire to change.

Intensity is a matter of how much you really want to change. If your focus is about the way you direct your energy, then your intensity is about the amount of energy you invest in changing. The Master of Change recognizes that it's his or her level of intensity that separates him or her from people who just lend lip service to change. If you are deeply desirous about changing your life for the better, then you had better check your personal intensity level, because your intensity level will always parallel your level of personal commitment. If you are totally committed to changing, then your intensity level runs high. If you approach change without great commitment, your intensity level will eventually run down. When it comes to your intensity, it must be just as great at the end of a project as it was in the beginning. That's why your level of commitment is so important. Commitment carries intensity with it to the very end of change. I have always enjoyed the question, "Why is a pig more committed than a chicken?" Because getting an egg from a chicken doesn't require nearly as much commitment as getting bacon from a pig! When it comes to your level of commitment to change, which one are you, a chicken or a pig?

Your **Resourcefulness** to create change requires you to take massive action. This is where you become proactive and go on the offense. This is the time when you explore all of your options and decide on the best course of action. This is where you engage the creative part of your mind and figure out a way…no matter what. What pressures are you prepared to bring to others or bear yourself to make things happen? How far are you willing to extend yourself, both physically and mentally? How many other people will you call upon to assist you in attaining your goals? What will you change about your behavior? I am certain that at this point you realize that if you do not alter your behavior and do so consistently, you will never make significant changes in your life. I suppose that brings us back to priorities again. If you really want it, you'll figure out a way. Perhaps the best examples of resourcefulness can be witnessed in children. Born as limitless human beings, they only learn what the word NO means from others. Because the word NO has so little meaning to them in their early years, they are incredibly persistent and resourceful, especially when it comes to getting something that they really want. I saw this in my own children as each holiday season approached. They would watch the television commercials that featured the latest, greatest and coolest toys and they would begin campaigning for the toys on a daily basis until we were worn down. Then low and behold, for the holidays they got what they wanted. Do you possess the resourcefulness of your youth? Well you can, if change is at the top of your priority list.

What can be said of **Enthusiasm** that has not already been said? People with an enthusiastic demeanor just seem to make things happen and enjoy life more. For the most part, people tend to come in two different attitude types. They either feel upbeat or feel beat up. Which one are you? Doom and gloom or ecstatic with all of the opportunities and possibilities that life has to offer? Enthusiasm is a choice. It's a choice that you can make right now and that choice will improve the rest of your life. I promise, it's a lot easier and a lot more fun to see all of the things that are right about the world, than dwell on the things that are wrong. Where you see is where you go. See life and people as good and that's what you get. See people and things as bad and that's what you get…every time!

By incorporating the F.I.R.E. concept into your life you will be able to create more positive change in your life and cope with or manage any change that life throws in your path. You will become an inspiration to others and your personal confidence will skyrocket. It has been said, "If a person is on fire, others will come just to see him/her burn." While not to be taken in the literal sense, figuratively speaking, passionate and inspired people bring out the best in themselves and in others.

Narrow your **Focus,** increase your level of **Intensity,** become more **Resourceful** and heighten your personal **Enthusiasm** on a daily basis. You will be amazed at how easy change becomes and how much fun you can have as you grow and inspire others.

Focus, Intensity, Resourcefulness and Enthusiasm are the keys to change.

Here's what you can do…

Only think about what you want.

Want only the best.

Either you are committed 100% or not at all!

LESSON 21

The Price of Change Comes in Many Forms

Earlier in the book we discussed that, when it comes to personal and professional change, there is always a price to pay. I thought it would be helpful if we explored some of the things you may have to give up in order for you to experience the changes that you want. The price you are going to have to pay will come in many forms. Some of the things you will have to give up will be commodities, such as time and money, while other sacrifices may come in the form of altered relationships and attitudinal and mental shifts. And if you are looking for significant change, it is quite possible that more than one price may have to be paid.

A few years ago I read a wonderful book that really puts life sacrifice in perspective. "Your Money Or Your Life" is a book that anyone who is serious about change must read. The book does an incredible job of helping identify what you are giving up, especially when it comes to the price we pay when we exchange time for money. While the price of change comes in many forms, in today's society most change involves paying the price of time, money or both. And, while both time and money are prized and valuable commodities, ultimately most people eventually come to the reality that money can be replaced, while time is always passing and is precious and irreplaceable. Each day when you go to work you are exchanging your time for money. When you go to the store to purchase something you exchange both time and money for goods. In order for the storekeeper to stock the item you purchased he or she had to purchase it from someone else. That process also took time and money. And so it goes, the great exchange. Something costs and someone pays. Occasionally what is paid is not always in the form of money. Very often, time or providing a service is exchanged for goods or other services or money. But, someone always pays and all things come with a cost.

The important thing to remember here is that changing your life requires an exchange. You give something up to get something else in exchange. Life has always been this way and it always will. And as easy as it is for you to appreciate that time and money are things that are often the price we have to pay for change, there is more to the price of change than meets the eye. Certainly there is more than time and money.

You may have to pay the price of an attitude shift. So much of who we are as individuals is visible in our attitudes. In order to evolve to a higher level, one of the changes you may have to make is how you view other people and the world in general. Part of your attitude has to do with your expectations. When it comes to your outlook on others and your universe, you pretty much get what you expect. The Master of Change understands that attitude often determines altitude. The more you maintain a consistently great attitude, the higher your level of success can be. When you pay the price of altering your attitude and expectations for the better, you dramatically improve the possibility of changing your life for the better.

You may have to change the quality of your personal behavior. Paying the price of giving up limiting or self-defeating behavior is often a difficult price to pay. Mostly because over time we convince ourselves that as good as we are is probably as good as we are ever going to be, so we settle and give up striving for excellence. The majority of our behavior is so habitual that the challenge of changing behavior often requires an enormous amount of focused attention and personal discipline. If you are in the habit of being late for appointments, to improve your life you need to give up the habit. If you procrastinate, get into the habit of doing things NOW. If the habit of biting your nails is negatively affecting your image, it's time to stop. Whatever the behavior, if it does not support you to attain what you want, stop it and replace it with a different behavior. This is where a Change Coach is so important, because it does help to have someone babysit you. All that matters is that you change, not how you change. The more someone can keep you aware of old behaviors, the more likely you are to shift to new and better behaviors. When it comes to changing behavior, the key is awareness. Remember, success is a habit and so is change. To create the habit of succeeding and changing, you must be prepared to face your fears, while at the same time, explore the limitless possibilities that lie before you. So pay great attention to both your mental as well as physical behavior. If you want to change, old behavior has to be replaced with new and different behavior.

You may have to pay the price of changing some of your relationships. This price to pay is a difficult one, because on some level you probably like most of the people in your life. Having said that, it's important for you to realize that not everyone in your life wants you to grow as a person or change who you are. Because so many people place such a high value on comfort, most tend to like things exactly as they are. Some of the people you believe to be your closest friends might not like you quite as much if your life's accomplishments surpassed theirs. People change and so do relationships. Sometimes in life it's just time to move on and leave some stale relationships behind. I encourage you to surround yourself with people who support you in your life goals; people who you feel good about contributing to your success as you contribute to theirs. Face it, there are some people who you are better off without. If so, conceive a method by which you put less energy into those relationships. They suck the life out of you and bring nothing to the table. Instead of elevating and supporting you, they will become human anchors and bring you down. This doesn't mean that you should thoughtlessly toss people out of your life, nor does it mean that, if you are in a miserable marriage which you have worked on repairing and cannot, you are doomed to a life of unhappiness. Move on and move on fast. Life was meant to be enjoyed and if that means that you have to change some relationships to enjoy it, well then change. And once you change, don't look back. You can learn from the past, but put your energy into where you are going, not where you have been.

That's why windshields are larger then rear view mirrors. Look where you are going because where you look is where you go.

For most, becoming a Master of Change demands that you pay the price of becoming a lot more confrontational. Now being more confrontational does not mean getting into a fight. It does mean that you may have to do a much better job of dealing with the feelings and emotions that hold you back. In short, your ability to confront is your willingness to deal with the truth about who you really are and how you deal with other people and situations. On a personal level you need to be honest about your fears, worries and anxieties. On a day-to-day level there is probably a laundry list of things you would like to say or do that you just shy away from. Why? Simple! People refuse to confront when they fear the reaction of others. And so, rather than live your life on your own terms, you alter your life and withhold your feelings because of how you believe others might react. How sad! I often wonder how different people would act, speak and behave if they knew that they couldn't fail and would not be rejected by others. Chances are, they would be totally different. In all likelihood, they would be true fearless warriors, ready, willing and able to handle any person and any challenge. And, while much has be written about the importance of learning to confront yourself and others, I must emphasize that becoming a person skilled at confrontation can change your life dramatically. So take some risk, speak up and let your feelings be known. Better to get the feelings and emotions out and run the risk of how people react, than keep the feelings and emotions inside and grow frustrated and disillusioned. Effectively dealing with people and life issues is always more difficult in your imagination than it is in reality.

If you explore your own life, I'm certain you will find other prices that you have paid beyond time, money, attitude, relationships and confrontation. This is the time to take inventory of what is keeping you where you are. Once you identify those obstacles, become determined to pay the price of change and overcome those roadblocks, you will live your life on different terms.

Be willing to exchange the life you are living for the life you want to live.

Here's what you can do…

Explore what lies beyond the life your presently live.

Take more risk.

Understanding comes from experience!

LESSON 22

You Learn When You Are Ready

One of the greatest influences in my life has been my stepfather, Jimmy Vassalotti. Jim and my mom just celebrated 30 years of marriage and everyone who knows Jimmy agrees that he is a really cool guy. An accomplished and successful architect and businessman, Jimmy knew the ways of the world. He has had a profound impact on my life as he shared with me his philosophy on everything from aging, life, finances and business to how to change in order to live life effortlessly. At 93, he continues to influence me and I am constantly amazed by how his knowledge has the ability to change how I think and feel. He always reminds me, "Wisdom comes with age." And as the years go on, I am more convinced than ever that he is right. This, of course, does not mean that just because you spend a lot of years on the planet that you are a sage, however, you have to admit that life is a great teacher.

As Jimmy aged, I realized that he often spent a great deal of his time in quiet thought. He would just sit and be focused on things beyond the activities in the room. One of the things that makes my relationship with Jimmy so special is the ability to discuss any subject. We had no limits on our conversations and no topic was ever out of bounds. So one day when we were alone, I asked him the question that was burning in my mind. "When you sit there alone and quiet, what are you thinking about?" I have always had a fascination with life and mortality, so I was curious about what a 93 year old thought about in his spare time, which is all he has, lots of spare time. Jimmy considered my question for a while and responded, "I think about how to make this a happy day!" There you have it…the wisdom of 93 years of living culled down into one insightful statement. It's not that he expected someone else to make it a happy day for him; he accepted the responsibility of making it a happy day for himself. I learned a lot that day and my life has been changed since.

If you are fortunate, you have someone like Jimmy in your life, someone who you can go to when you need to learn the lessons of life. For a significant part of my life, Jimmy has been my Change Coach and is still a mentor. Unfortunately, not everyone is willing to seek the wisdom of others and take the time to learn the lessons of life. As a result, they often live unfulfilled lives that cause them great frustration. In order for you to change, you have to be willing to learn. Basically there are only two ways to learn: you can learn on your own through experiences or you can learn through the experiences of others. Both ways work, however, learning on your own can often be time consuming and painful. What amazes me is how much we could learn if we had the courage to admit that we didn't know everything and were willing to take the time and ask. The majority of information you need to improve your life is readily available. You probably have access to some caring people who are eager to help you reach your goals.

When we were children, our parents often told us things that they thought we should know about making it through life with the least amount of stress possible. I know my parents did and hopefully your parents did too. Unfortunately, like most people, especially young people, I just thought I had all the answers. I actually believed that I knew all there was to know and didn't need the help of others. Well, wisdom often does come with age and as I got older, I realized the wealth of information my parents and others possess. I now cherish the wisdom of others and seek out their life experiences whenever possible. It's just easier.

In life, you learn when you are ready and not a moment sooner. The good news is that there is always something to learn and always someone willing to teach. Most important, because information is always readily available, it's never too late to learn. When the day arrives that you come to the realization that you do not have all of the answers, you are on your way to creating the kind of changes that can improve the rest of your life. The more you are willing to seek out better ways to change, the faster you will arrive at your goals with less stress. You do not have to experience the experience to learn, you can gain experience from others. But, you have to want the knowledge. When my son Peter was ready to leave for college, we had to get his car and his personal possessions from Park City, Utah, to Long Island, New York, about 2,300 miles. So here we were driving cross-country together. What a tremendous opportunity for a father and son to bond, to share feelings and emotions, to reminisce about the past and discuss the limitless possibilities of the future. At one point in the trip, Peter decided to take a nap. As I drove on in silence and looked over at him sleeping, it occurred to me that the most influence I was going to have on Peter had already occurred during his first eighteen years. Was he really prepared for living alone? Was he up to the daily decisions that he would have to make? Had I given him enough information for him to begin this new chapter of his life? I wasn't sure. So when he awoke, I started to ask him about his life goals. Much to my pleasure, he seemed very clear about what he wanted to accomplish in his lifetime. Yet, still believing that I could contribute something to the equation, I asked him the following question, "What would you like to know?" To which he responded, "What do you mean?" So I went on. "About life, what would you like to know about life?" To which he responded, "Nothing." I said, "Are you sure, I know about a lot of things." And Peter said, " No, I'm okay." Here I was, driving along with nothing I would rather do than share the wisdom of years and the secrets of life with my son, but he was just not ready to learn. A golden opportunity and at age 18 he actually thought he knew it all. Oh well, you learn when you are ready. Perhaps in time he will come to realize that others can help him through life easier than he might be able to do it on his own. The Master of Change is always seeking information: the more that is learned, the more one continues to evolve to a higher level.

You learn when you are ready…every day on this earth is

another day to learn. If you learn something each day, you are growing and changing for the better. Learn nothing in a day…you have wasted a day of your life. A true Master of Change learns throughout his or her life.

If you are serious about change, keep learning and thinking about how you can make each day a happy day.

Here's what you can do…

Get involved in lifelong learning.

Choose to enjoy each day.

Happiness
is a
gift you
give
yourself...

LESSON 23

Image Impacts Change

If you want to change your life, you'd better be prepared to change your image. A great deal of what it takes to change your life has to do with the image you project. Not just the way you perceive yourself, but the image that others have of you. It has been said that image is perception. I am inclined to agree. What people see when they see you is their perception and their perception has a lot to do with how they respond to you. So if you want to change your life, you must consider how to improve the way people perceive you. The effect that a great image has on others is often referred to as the "Halo Effect." A great image elevates you in the eyes of the people with whom you come into contact. Studies actually do indicate that your personal appearance has an enormous impact on others. The more attractive the image, the more you project the image of success and prosperity in the eyes of others.

I suppose the big question you must ask yourself as part of your decision to change is, "How do I want to be perceived?" So much has been written about how another person's perception of you is their reality and how you perceive yourself is your reality. The good news is that you can make a conscious decision to change your image, and therefore, you can change how you feel about yourself and how the people in your world feel about you. Changing your image is a skill that anyone can learn. And there has never been a better time for you to learn than now, so I thought you would appreciate some ideas you can use to enhance your image.

Your image must be consistent with what you want to be. If your goal is to be taken more seriously in business, then you must change your image so that it is consistent with how you want to be perceived. If you want to be perceived as a more powerful and persuasive person, your image must become one that reflects the image of power. Depending on your life situation and the image you want to project, you have to be prepared to alter your image so that it matches the situation. The moment you are willing to change your appearance/image for the better, you will gain status, increase your level of professionalism and improve your opportunities in life and in business. Because when you change your image for the better, you increase your personal and professional credibility. And when your credibility increases, your level of personal power and persuasiveness improves. As a result, your opportunity to become more successful is greatly enhanced. Then all you have to do is take advantage of those opportunities. Opportunity does not knock once. If you pay attention, you will realize that opportunity is knocking all the time. All you have to do is take action and respond positively to alter your destiny.

Because changing your image is a learned skill, people who want to alter how they are perceived and are willing to invest some time and money can change how others view them. Once you decide to change your image, you need to determine exactly what image you want to project. Only when you are clear about how you want to be perceived can you take the necessary steps to reinvent yourself.

Very often changing your image cannot be done alone. You may require some assistance when it comes to assessing how others view you. Go to the people you respect, people who will tell you the truth about how you come across to others, and ask their opinion. If they understand that you want this information because you want to change for the better, they will help you. Then listen to what they have to say. Don't defend, just listen. Even if their feedback and/or criticism hurts your feelings, just listen. Without accurate feedback, you cannot change.

Then start acting on that feedback and continue to change until you look different, feel different and begin to act differently. You will be amazed at how differently people will respond to you.

Some important things to remember about your image:

1. You can never create a business that is bigger than the image you project. For that reason alone, you must be constantly aware of how others view you. The more you want to succeed in any area of life, the more committed you must be to consistently changing and expanding your image as you expand your goals.
2. A winning image increases your powers of persuasive-

ness. The more persuasive your image, the more effective you will be in personal and professional situations. People will be more responsive to you.

3. Whatever a person sees when they see you must be equal to or better than what they imagined you to be or they will be disappointed. We all create pictures in our mind about other people prior to meeting them. We come with expectations of others and others come with expectations about us. If your image fails the "First Impact" test, there is almost nothing that can be done to salvage the relationship or undo the disappointment. Visual impact very often determines your personal power and credibility.
4. The image you project has a direct and indelible impression on the mind of others and can alter the opinions they have about you, your success, your relationships and your lifestyle.
5. Your image must be consistently excellent. You are only as good as your last impression. That is how you will be judged. Remember, your appearance is a tool. It makes a statement, either positive or negative, about all that you represent. Your appearance can be used to dramatically change every aspect of your life. There is a big difference between looking your very best and looking okay. You always know the difference and so do the people who observe you.
6. Your personal charisma is tied directly to your image. If your image goes down the drain, your charisma goes with it. People will make decisions about you based on what they see, not necessarily what you say. So what they see has to be more than they imagined and create a positive

impact. That means, as part of your commitment to change, you may have to change the style in which you dress. Face it; some of your closets should be cleaned with a flame thrower or hand grenade. You may have to alter your hairstyle or hair color, makeup and accessories. Besides the obvious neat and clean, here are some things that really go a long way to increasing the way others view you: your wristwatch, shoes, attaché case, jewelry and pen. Start changing your accessories and appearance and you will further change your life.

And, while the reasons for you to improve your image are limitless, it basically comes down to three things:

1. You will increase your confidence.
2. You will gain more admiration, recognition and respect.
3. It will become easier for you to become more successful.

To change who you are, you must act and look like the person you want to be.

So each day before you leave your home, ask yourself the following question, "Am I projecting an image of the old me, or do I represent the person I am committed to becoming?"

Regardless of what you desire, your personal image must be larger than your vision.

Here's what you can do...

Invest in your image…it's worth it.

Be your best each day.

THINGS THAT ARE ALWAYS CHANGING:

Tide

Temperature

Weather

Clouds

Rivers

Fashion

Fads

Attitudes

Technology

Feelings

Body

Spirit

Mood

Time

IN A UNIVERSE WHERE EVERYTHING IS CHANGING, ARE YOU?

LESSON 24

Change Happens When You Do

Because you are your own perception and because you have the freedom to see yourself as anything you want, you can control the rate in which you change. The moment you decide to view yourself in a different way, you become a different person and your life changes forever. That means replacing the old you with a reinvented you. Change happens when you do and if you want, you can make change happen in an instant. To become a Master of Change you must first become the master of your "NOW." Your NOW is really all that you have immediate control over. With no control over your past and no guarantee of the future, managing the moment is crucial!

Change happens when you say so and as long as you are committed to changing. What time could possibly be better than NOW? That means you have the ability to change your attitude, image, appearance, communication skills, level of confrontation, personal and professional habits NOW. Not tomorrow, not next week and not next year, but NOW. Change NOW and everything else in your world changes immediately.

Change happens when you are ready; everyone's rate of readiness is different. If you are serious about improving your life, start creating the changes you want NOW. You know that you want to make your life better and you also know that you can control your rate of change. So what are you waiting for? There has never been a better time for you to take control of your life and change it than NOW. As always, you are in the driver's seat. It's ***YOU*** who must determine exactly how much change you want in your life and how fast you want those changes to occur. For the majority of people, change occurs at two distinct rates. You can change in an incremental or gradual way OR you can go for bold, dramatic and outrageous change. If you have opted for outrageous change, you are committed to changing NOW.

And, while most people would like the effects of instant, outrageous change, they tend to wind up changing incrementally because incremental change represents safety and comfort. The higher the value you place on safety and comfort the more tempted you are to keep things the same. Of course, incremental change is better than remaining stuck in sameness, just keep in mind that while you are taking your time changing, the clock of life keeps ticking. So, get on with it and change who you are. The minute you change yourself all other change will follow the new you. Oh, I'm sure there are times when incremental or gradual change may make the most sense, but if you are interested in a life filled with adventure and opportunity, go for change in the NOW. Get outrageous!

Changing who you are as a person, in an outrageous fashion, takes great courage and the willingness to get into the pain of change and personal growth. We are talking about a lot more than changing your wardrobe; we are talking about the determination you possess to totally transform who you are by altering how you look, how you think and how you behave. Changing in an outrageous way requires a conscious thought. Once you make that decision it becomes the catalyst that drives you to a better quality life. Outrageous change happens when you decide that it does. It is the end result of your personal resolve, your grit, your guts, your gall and your chutzpah…COURAGE.

If you have opted for dramatic, instant and outrageous change, you must begin by thinking about what you think about. No more knee jerk reaction to people and situations. Because thoughts have power and energy, what you think about is what you will bring about. For that reason, you have to examine the mindset in which you process information. Because we are creatures of habit, your first instinct may not necessarily be your best instinct. That could just be your habit. To really accelerate change, big time change, you must come from the position that all of the thoughts and instincts that you have right now need to be re-thought. This requires you to begin to live in the world of more, new, better and different. It also means that you must be willing to take more risk and stop seeking safety in your decisions and actions.

In the world of more, new, better and different, nothing is sacred and everything is subject to change. Here's how it works. The next time you are about to do something, run through the list of more, new, better and different. "Is there a new way for me to do this Should I be doing more of this? Can I do this better? Is there a different way to do this?" All success and change comes from entertaining the thoughts of more, new, better and different. When you alter your thinking and embrace the idea that all things can be approached differently, then you are on your way to outrageous change.

Change happens when you start living in the world of new, more, better and different because then you are forced to examine every aspect of your life. You will realize that just because things have been done a certain way, regardless of how long they have been done that way, does not mean that they have to stay that way forever. You can change things, you can make things newer, and you can have more and do more. You can live a better life. Every area of your life can be different and improved.

Change follows people like a magnet. You change and your world changes. Outrageous change occurs in the NOW. NOW is the time to make your life happen. Just live each day and process all information and decisions through the concepts of more, new, better and different.

You change your life and make things happen by exploring what can be done newer, more, better and differently.

Here's what you can do…

Be courageous in your change making.

Get outrageous.

As soon as you change, your world changes.

LESSON 25

Live the Four C's

Practically everyone knows at least one person who has made a dramatic transition in his or her life. If you don't, surely you have heard the stories of how seemingly ordinary people harness extraordinary energy, literally transforming themselves in such a spectacular way that it is impossible not to notice. These Masters of Change can and should represent great role models for what is possible when you set your focus on creating a better life for yourself.

Throughout my life, I have witnessed major life transformations in so many people who have all demonstrated four life-changing traits. These four traits, which all Masters of Change have in common, are essential for you to adopt if you are determined to improve the quality of your life. These change artists are the people who you should look to for inspiration and motivation. Their ability to change should serve as proof positive of what you can accomplish, when you totally invest all of your heart, mind, body and spirit into changing.

The Four C's:

1. ***Character***
2. ***Courage***
3. ***Commitment***
4. ***Confrontation***

These four personal traits must become your cornerstones of transition. They must permeate your thoughts and behavior in such a way that they impact all of your actions and decision-making, each and every day. Being involved in personal and professional change is like being in a huge tug-of-war. There is the part of you that wants and knows that to improve your life you have to change, and there is the old you, the habit that keeps pulling you back to the way things used to be. This tug-of-war occurs in all people who work toward change. It's the constant battle of what you aspire to be versus what you have always been. **The only way you can win the war and win it *PERMANENTLY* is by consistently monitoring your personal character, your courage, your commitment and your confrontational skills.**

Your ***character*** is the essence of who you are as a person and what you stand for. In life, especially when it comes to personal and professional change, your ***character*** is the critical element that carries you from initial concept to completion. ***Character*** comes into play when you give your word to yourself and others about the changes you are about to make. Make those changes and your ***character*** remains intact. Fail to make those changes and your ***character*** erodes. Staying true to what you say is a habit and so is failing to remain true to your word. If your character fails, your personal integrity follows. The next thing that happens is that you fall into the habit of not being true to who you are and what you aspire to be. After that, change becomes extremely difficult to create. George Eliot was quoted as saying, "Change is destiny." Well, if change is your destiny you are going to need great strength of character. An individual with strong personal character can accomplish great things and is virtually limitless in his or her ability to improve his or her life. People of great character are people of high energy, constantly moving forward in the direction of their dreams. They consistently do what is right. Their determination enables them to win and change for the better.

For profound change, there is just no substitute for courage. The courageous person is willing to face the challenge of changing everything about his or her life. The challenge to change becomes a highly personal issue and because of his or her determination, courageous people simply refuse to lose. They are fearless and tireless in their pursuit of excellence. Although they recognize that change can be intimidating, they press forward, not allowing the emotion of fear to deter them. They also recognize that, in most instances, staying the same can hurt them deeply. When your fear of staying the same is greater than whatever fear you have of changing, you change. Every day and in all that you do, your courage must keep you on the course of change, regardless of the temptation you feel to revert back to old behaviors, which have been thrown in your path to keep you mediocre, average and comfortable. Your job is to fight those feelings, even though they are real and frightening. Your personal resolve to break out of your old habits must be so great that you find the will power to change, no matter what. Your courage must now become part of the new character you are developing on your way to a better life.

Eventually, you will be able to measure your life accomplishments based on your level of commitment. And, while your level of personal commitment has a great deal to do with the actions that you take, being a person of great commitment has much to do with the words that you use. If you are determined to change, your words become the tools that measure your level of commitment.

SOON has to be replaced with NOW.

CAN has to be replaced with WILL.

COULD & SHOULD get replaced with MUST.

DO replaces TRY.

NOW, WILL, MUST and DO are powerful words of change and commitment. The moment these words of commitment become part of your every day vocabulary, the closer you come to attaining your life goals. These words must become your verbal weapons of choice in the war to change. The more weapons you have at your disposal the better. Ultimately, you will be judged by what you do, not merely your intent. Get into the habit of doing things NOW, not SOON. It's not what you CAN do that matters; it's what you WILL do that changes your life. Change is not about what you COULD or SHOULD do, it's what you MUST do. And success is about what you do, not what you try to do.

You can TRY to change from now until forever; all that matters is what you DO!

NOW, WILL, MUST and DO are words of confidence and certainty. And the more confident and certain you are about the changes you want to make, the easier it becomes to elevate your level of ***commitment.*** **Commitment and Certainty are the Twin C's of change.** Show me someone with ***commitment*** and I will show you an individual with crystal clear ***certainty.*** Show me someone with laser beam ***certainty*** and I will show you a person of powerful ***commitment.*** The words you select and the actions you take must be consistent with your desire to change. All of your words must be steeped in ***certainty*** and all of your actions and decisions must be steeped in ***commitment.*** So choose your words carefully. They reflect your intent and ***commitment*** to improve your life.

People willing to be confrontational have a greater opportunity to change their lives because confrontation creates change. The amount of change you experience is often directly tied to just how confrontational you become. Becoming more confrontational indicates that you are really desirous of changing. Unfortunately, many people who want to change for the better get bogged down at the confrontation step of change. Their fear of how others may respond to them or what they say or do prevent them from effectively dealing with important issues and they remain stuck. ***Confrontation demands courage***. The more courageous you become, the higher your level of confrontation will be. Once you master the skill of confrontation you will be able to deal with the truth about yourself and others. Then, and only then, will you be on your way to massive and irreversible change. And, while the truth can very often be painful, unless you get into the pain of truth, you will remain stuck in your circle of sameness. Confrontation requires the commitment and certainty to change, as well as large doses of personal courage and character. The more courage, commitment and character you possess, the more confidence you will have when it comes time for you to confront a person or situation. Start confronting some of the issues that you have been tolerating. You will feel a lot better about yourself and your future.

Character, courage, commitment and confrontation are the tools of change.

Here's what you can do…

Do what you say you are going to do.

Face the truth about who you are.

TASTES CHANGE

I used to like tomatoes…not anymore.

Hated mushrooms…love them now.

Liked pets and had a bunch of them… no longer a pet person.

Was an avid baseball fan…the game is just too slow for my taste.

Always needed the next cool car… my old cars are just fine.

Wouldn't read a book…cannot read enough.

Needed to dine out…prefer dinner at home.

Spend, Spend, Spend…Save, Save, Save.

Couldn't watch basketball…love the game.

School is a waste of time…always looking to learn.

Liked golf as a teen…too busy for golf…passionate about golf.

Was a taker…now a giver.

Big city guy…small town guy.

**HOW ABOUT YOU?
WHAT HAVE YOU CHANGED
RECENTLY?**

LESSON 26

Manage Your Emotions

Skiing the glacier in Chamonix, France, seemed like a great idea at the time. For an intermediate skier, this seemed like the adventure of a lifetime and it was. At an elevation of almost 12,000 feet, the air was thin, breathing was difficult and the weather was changing for the worse. I was part of a four-person expedition that was led by an experienced mountain guide. Skiing on a glacier was a new and intimidating experience for me. Surrounded by crevasses and extremely challenging terrain, I was being physically and emotionally pushed to the max. And for a while, things were going pretty well, until the storm blew in. When the weather cleared, I found myself separated from the rest of the party. Alone and lost in a never-ending field of white, I was on the edge of panic; I decided to push on in the direction I thought the others had gone. After miles of trekking through the snow, with no one in sight and gasping for air, I was ready to give up and lie down in the snow to die. I just couldn't push ahead any further. Confronted with the choices of quit or press on, I found a hidden reserve of energy and turned my fear and panic into resolve and determination. To this day I'm not sure if I found the search party or the search party found me, but it was as terrifying an event as I have ever experienced. While all of this was taking place, I was acutely aware of my two choices; I could either let my emotions get the best of me OR I could get the best of my emotions.

A big part of creating change in your life has to do with your emotions and how you respond to the situations that occur in your life. Your ability to effectively manage how you handle life events is an integral part of being able to change the circumstances of your life. Notice that the name of this lesson <u>is not</u> Control Your Emotions, it's Manage Your Emotions. Because there will be times in your life when you are so emotionally overwhelmed that your reaction and response may be simply beyond your control. The goal of this lesson is about what you do after the initial shock of what has occurred to you. This is about management of your demeanor and taking charge of your life.

It was Sunday evening August 17, 1997, and we just returned home from a family dinner. As usual, when we entered the kitchen we went to the answering machine to check for messages. There was only one message that night. My sister Cyndy, who lives in Florida, had called and asked me to call as soon as I got home. I could almost tell from the sound of her voice that something was wrong and when she answered the phone my heart dropped. Her words, "Daddy's dead" sent me into shock. My father, the best friend a person could have, had died suddenly of a heart attack. No warning, no history, no hospitalization…nothing! One minute he was here and in apparent great health and the next minute he was gone. And, while I logically understood that everyone had to die sooner or later and recognized that he was getting on in years, I was still emotionally unprepared for his passing. He had been so healthy and full of life that I couldn't comprehend that he was gone. In a flash, everything in my life had changed, and for those of you who have had similar experiences, you know exactly what I am speaking about. In fact, it's only after years that I am even able to write or speak about his loss without crying.

Your emotions can change in a moment and when they do, the challenge you face is to manage how you respond to life changing events. There was nothing I could do about my initial shock and the total devastation my family was experiencing, but there was a lot I could do about the events that followed. With tremendous discipline and control I had to get myself together and figure out how to get my family to Florida by morning, then finalize all of the necessary arrangements for my Dad's funeral. Plus, I wanted to write a eulogy that would make him proud and present it without falling apart. The day was an emotionally draining blur, but when I look back, it was just the way he would have wanted it to be. And the only way we were able to make things happen, despite feelings running high, was by managing our emotions. Easy? Not necessarily, but if you want to change your life, you must be able to control how events affect you.

While all people are emotional about one thing or another, levels of emotion vary, as do how people express their emotions. Everyone eventually realizes that they will be faced with emotionally trying times during their life. The keys to managing your emotions, rather than allowing your emotions to determine your behavior, are focus and discipline. The more focused you become on what needs to be done, despite the circumstances that surround you, the more apt you will be to control your response and do what is necessary. Mentally, this demands that you use tremendous discipline in looking beyond the challenge you are faced with, as you steadfastly take those actions that will get you closer to resolving your problem. As my good friend Richard Flint says, **"All decisions pass through your emotions on the way to your brain."**

As with most things in life, you have choices. In highly emotional situations, your choices are fight or fold. You can either do what is necessary to get past the initial emotional trauma or you can go down the drain, in which case you become part of the problem rather than the solution. The person who aspires to be a true Master of Change understands that what happens to you in life is not nearly as important as how you respond to what happens to you in life. Some things will always remain beyond your control. Your challenge is to always remain in control of the only thing you have instant and total control over…your ability to respond affirmatively to life's challenges. Emotional change presents you with an extraordinary opportunity for personal growth. Be certain to take advantage of the opportunity. Face it, change IS going to happen! Your best bet is to accept what life hands you and make it work to your advantage.

Manage your emotions or your emotions will manage you. It's your choice.

Here's what you can do…

Act rather than react.

Do what needs to be done.

EMBRACE CHANGE AND MAKE IT WORK TO YOUR ADVANTAGE...

LESSON 27

Make Money Your Slave

One of the ways you can change your life is by getting your financial world in order. I am sure you would agree that while most people want more money, regardless of how much they have, very few people invest the time to learn how to create a better financial future. This lesson contains the basics on money management. The strategies and actions I recommend are easy to follow. If you are prepared to change the way you view and manage money, this lesson will change the rest of your life. As previously discussed, everyone wants more or less of something. Well, when it comes to money, I still have not met a person who wants less. This lesson explains how you can accumulate more money...**SERIOUS MONEY.**

First of all, if you want to change your financial future, it's probably a good idea to read some books about money. The book that changed my financial life was, "The Richest Man In Babylon" by George S. Clason. This book is easy and enjoyable to read and because it's told in parable form, it makes for a fun way to learn how to make your money work for you. I know what you are thinking about now…"How can I possibly get out of the financial situation I am in, no less become financially independent?" Well, you can make money your slave, regardless of how much you earn or what you presently have saved, even if you have saved nothing. The book "The Millionaire Next Door" does an extraordinary job of detailing how people who are not high earners can become wealthy. And Robert Kiyosaki's "Rich Dad, Poor Dad" is loaded with great information on changing your financial situation. Yes, it takes time and discipline, but it can be done and ***YOU*** can do it. Make the decision to do some reading about how you can alter your financial destiny.

If you want to change your financial future, the time to get started is NOW. If you believe that Social Security is going to be adequate for you to live on at the time of retirement, forget it. The reality is that it's up to you to make the decisions that will provide for your own financial future. **Remember, you cannot retire on excuses.** When you retire, all of your reasons and justifications as to why your financial condition is not better will not matter. So the sooner you begin to look beyond your present financial condition and plan for the future, the better. The fact that you may be in a sorry financial condition today has nothing to do with what you can create tomorrow. The faster you create and implement your wealth plan, the better. That's right, you need a plan. Without a debt reduction and wealth accumulation plan you are doomed to failure. Your financial habits have created your present financial condition. Unless you are prepared to create new habits, you will continue down the path you are presently on. A debt reduction and wealth accumulation plan becomes the foundation of establishing new financial behaviors. Only by changing your behavior can you dramatically improve your financial future.

When I was a child, the cost of riding the subway system in New York City was a nickel. My grandmother, who was a terrific financial manager, had a very clear philosophy on money. Simply stated, Grandma's philosophy was, "If you see a penny, pick it up because you can't get on the train with 4 cents." There you have it, the wisdom of the ages. All money matters; small denominations can become larger denominations. Grandma's philosophy is in sharp contrast to the new twist on the old adage, "A penny saved is a penny earned," which has become, "A penny saved is a waste of time." The issue here has nothing to do with the penny, but rather how you view money. All money counts and if you learn how to eliminate debt and accumulate money, you can make your money work for you instead of you working for money. What money can provide you with is the freedom to make better life choices. No I am not suggesting that money is the only thing that matters in life or that money can buy happiness. But money can buy a Ferrari so you can drive around looking for happiness. More money can change your life because money gives you more choices.

In order for you to accumulate more money, you need a plan. Christopher Columbus died broke. He didn't know where he was going, he didn't know where he was when he got there and he didn't know where he had been when he returned. YOU NEED A PLAN. My plan is rather simple and has worked for me as well as other people who I have coached toward financial independence. It's based on the philosophy of debt reduction and wealth accumulation, and that's the philosophy I want you to adopt. Wealth is more than a matter of money; it's a matter of attitude as is becoming debt free. Becoming wealthy begins with a major shift in how you think and act. And the great thing is, anyone can follow this Seven-Step plan.

My Seven-Step Wealth Plan:

Step 1 - ***Open A Wealth Account***
Step 2 - ***Maximize Your Earnings***
Step 3 - ***Spend Less Money***
Step 4 - ***Create A Debt Reduction Plan***
Step 5 - ***Create A Wealth Accumulation Plan***
Step 6 - ***Find A Great Financial Planner***
Step 7 - ***Never Deviate From The Plan***

Step 1—Open a wealth account. Don't question, just do it. That's right, go to your local bank and open a money market account that bears interest and gives you check writing privileges. When asked how you would like your checks to read, I suggest as follows. On the line below your name, in capitals have the words "WEALTH ACCOUNT" printed. The minute you walk out of the bank you will already feel better about your financial future. Attaining financial freedom has a great deal to do with your intent, and having a WEALTH ACCOUNT immediately indicates what your intent is. The money that will eventually be deposited into this account is sacred and can NEVER be used for anything other than earning you more money. This requires a lot of discipline. Most people are pretty good at the beginning of accumulation, when there isn't much in the account, but as the account balance begins to grow, you are going to be tempted to withdraw it for something that you believe you cannot live without. DO NOT TOUCH THE MONEY! This is the beginning of your financial freedom; so in the face of enormous temptation, remain strong.

Step 2—Maximize your earnings. Makes perfect sense, doesn't it? Just make more money. Well it's not all that simple. Plenty of high earners manage to have no money at time of retirement and a great many average earners are wealthy at this time. So maximizing your earnings is important, but how you manage what you earn is the critical step in wealth accumulation. However, your goal is to maximize your income. Nobody ever said you had to spend your life in the same job or career. Nothing stops you from exploring your earning options and finding new opportunities to generate more revenue. Start looking and approach increasing your income with a "Whatever it takes" attitude. If it means you have to make some bold changes, like changing jobs, taking a second job or asking for a raise, DO IT! This is a book about change, so change! If you want to make money your slave, you are going to need some money. It's your responsibility to explore every opportunity available, so be resourceful and creative.

Step 3—Spend less money. Duh! Let's see, if you earn more money and spend less money, you will have money to invest in your future. And, while this is rather elementary, most people just refuse to grasp the concept. Well, spending less money is tougher on some people than others. The reality is that spending is a habit and in the "buy now, pay later" world that we live in it's often difficult to stop spending. Amazing how our society has resorted to a plastic credit card to exist and how easy it is to spend. We overspend on credit because we refuse to believe that plastic is money. It's the same reason you are given plastic chips in exchange for "real money" in gambling casinos. If you gambled with actual currency, you wouldn't gamble as much, so we are given plastic chips, which we seldom treat like "real money." And because it is so easy to overspend, we wind up in debt. Not a good way to live. Imagine living a life that is debt free? You can. However, you are going to have to bite the bullet and STOP SPENDING. Along the way, start cutting up your credit cards as soon as you pay them off. Ultimately you should only have two credit cards. An American Express or Diners Club card or something comparable and a Visa or MasterCard. And from this minute forth, you never charge more than you can PAY IN FULL at the end of the month. No more interest charges carried forward from month to month. Banks continue to get rich on your lack of planning and discipline, while you stay mired in debt. Yes, I want you to enjoy life and live a balanced existence, but if all you have to show for all of your work is your lifestyle, you will work until you drop dead. I know plenty of high earners who live from month to month and don't have a penny in the bank. Just plain stupid! Stop spending.

Step 4—Create a debt reduction plan. Being a debtor is a habit, a mindset, just like becoming wealthy. With time and discipline practically everyone can work their way out of debt, regardless of how much they owe. This is the plan that worked well for me and, if you are committed to becoming debt free, it can work for you, too. Begin by making a list of all of your debt, starting with the smallest debt first and ending with the largest debt you have. This list should include all installment loans, leases, student loans, and personal loans, past taxes and mortgages…everything. Put the book down and do this now, even though this exercise may make you nauseous. Make the list. Once your list is complete and you have regained consciousness, there are two things that must happen, no matter what. First, DO NOT TAKE ON ANY NEW DEBT. That's right, no new debt. All that you owe is all that there is. Do not pile anything else on. Second, START PAYING OFF YOUR SMALLEST DEBT FIRST. You are going to do this by staying current with all of your other debt and at the same time diverting every available extra dollar you have toward reducing the smallest debt you have. This means you have to figure out a way to live on less as you work diligently to earn more. Starting now, 10% of your gross earnings gets dedicated toward debt reduction. Just do it! Take down one debt at a time, then the monthly payment that you no longer have to make plus 10 % of your gross earnings are applied to eliminating your next smallest debt. Systematically and over time your debt load will diminish. The idea of paying off your smallest debt first will give you tremendous gratification and get you into the habit of becoming debt free. You will love the way you feel when you pay something off and never have to pay it again.

Step 5—Create a wealth accumulation plan. The beginning of the plan calls for you to consistently save 10% of your gross income. That 10% gets deposited into your WEALTH ACCOUNT on a regular basis. And just to make sure you don't miss, you may want to arrange for this 10% to be automatically withheld and forwarded to your bank. About now you are thinking that I am either brilliant or totally nuts. Let's be honest, you think I'm nuts. You are asking yourself the following question. "If I am having a tough time making it on 100% of my earnings, how can I survive on 80%?" (10% for debt reduction and 10% for wealth accumulation.) "And I still have to pay taxes." Just trust me, you will. If your business cut your income by 20%, you would figure out a way to survive. Well, figure it out. The ultimate goal being, when you are completely out of debt, 20% of whatever you earn goes to savings. Savings is a habit just like spending and once you get into the habit of accumulation and watch your balance increase, you will take tremendous pride in what you have accomplished. Remember, all money counts, so don't fall into the "It doesn't matter" mentality. In other words, if you earn $500.00 a week, "How is saving $50 dollars going to make me wealthy?" Properly invested, money gives birth to more money. Just put the money away and don't touch it.

Step 6— Find a great financial planner. Your financial planner must be someone you trust, have rapport with, who is willing to take the time to understand what you want to accomplish and sells you nothing! Your financial planner becomes your financial change coach and must be prepared to support you in your plan and show you how to safely maximize your investments. The goal is to have your money earn interest and the interest on that money earns more interest. This way your money is always working for you. Even when you are asleep, your money is working for you. In order for your financial planner to be accurate and effective, he or she is going to need to know a lot about your finances and lifestyle, especially how you want to live at the time of retirement. So be prepared to do some research and answer some questions about your future goals. While your financial planner can show you the way to achieve your financial goals, ultimately it's up to you to carry out the plan. A good financial planner will also make certain that you have a current and registered Last Will and Testament as well as Trusts whenever indicated. And it's probably a good idea to have a back-up financial plan, because as you already know…things change.

Step 7—NEVER DEVIATE FROM THE PLAN. Oh, you will be tempted, but stay the course. You will see things you want to own, just stay the course. People will come to you with get rich quick opportunities, just stay the course. Your plan will only work to the extent that you work it. Never deviate from your plan. I'm speaking about 100% commitment, not 99%, but 100%. Anything short of total commitment will create disappointment, frustration and failure. Stay the course. Steps 1-6 will only matter if you adhere to step 7. NEVER DEVIATE FROM THE PLAN.

Making money your slave demands that you change your behavior and start thinking on a different level. Imagine what your life will be like when you have no debt and significant savings invested at a nice interest rate. And the money created from that interest would be enough to support your future lifestyle. Sure, you can still work if you want to, but wouldn't it be nice to know that you have the choice?

You determine your financial destiny.

Here's what you can do…

Get out of debt NOW!

Save, Save, Save.

You live in a world of unlimited financial possibilities…

LESSON 28

Find Out What's Possible

In order to effectively change your life, you have to determine what's possible. Finding out what's possible requires that you increase your level of awareness and begin to explore your personal potential. Only when you know what you can achieve can you construct a plan that will enable you to attain your goals. Finding out what is possible is another instance where the quality of your decision-making has a very powerful impact on your future. And, while everyone's personal and professional potential is different, your job is to identify what your maximum potential is. The goal here is to first identify what's possible for you and then to consistently move in the direction of achieving your personal best. Finding out what's possible has nothing to do with what others are capable of accomplishing. And, while the accomplishments of others can serve as inspiration and fuel your competitive nature, finding out what your maximum potential is and working toward your desired outcome is all that matters. An important factor to keep in mind is that you create your own standards. As long as you are honest with yourself, ***you will succeed.***

So as long as you get to set your own standards and BIG THINKING IS FREE, use your creative mind and let your imagination run free. Your personal potential is as large or as small as you imagine it to be. See yourself as someone with unlimited potential and life changing opportunities will present themselves. See yourself as stuck and limited and that is exactly what you will attract into your life, more of what you already have.

If you are uncertain about what's possible for you, start looking around. Increasing your awareness about the things around you will help you begin to decide in which direction you should move. Then ask yourself some questions about what you really want and the price you would have to pay to get what you want. When you ask the right questions of yourself and listen to your inner voice, you get all the information you need to make the right decisions about your future. In most instances, innately you already know the answer to any question you can ask yourself about your potential. For additional feedback about your potential, it's probably a good idea to get the opinions of others. But only ask people you trust to be honest with you and are big thinkers by nature. This is not the time to seek out limited thinking individuals. Because we tend to limit our possibilities, others are likely to see us in a greater light than we do ourselves.

A significant part of change has to do with the images you create in your mind. It has been said, "Seeing is believing" and while there is much to be said for visual evidence, "Believing is seeing" is the way to go. Once you believe with all of your heart that you can change your life, you will. The more you are willing to put the mental energy into images you want, the closer you get to maximizing your potential. Because changing the quality of your life has so much to do with your beliefs and your level of self worth, it is essential that you see yourself as deserving a better life than the one you are presently living. Only then can you let your imagination run free. And because our mind works in visual images, I use a dream board to continually remind me of my direction. Every time I have wanted to change my life, I have done so through pictures. Using magazines and brochures, I start clipping out the images of what I want or how I want to live and paste them on a giant size poster board. Start creating your dream board today and spend as much time as possible looking at it. When you do, imagine yourself living the life that your dream board represents. This simple and fun exercise can change your life. The more you are willing to see yourself changing for the better, the closer you come to reaching your potential.

Finding out what's possible for you to accomplish goes much further than considering a different life for you. Discovering your personal potential demands that you change your thinking from limited to limitless and from not worthy to incredibly deserving. In life, you ultimately get what you see yourself being worthy of. The more you believe you are entitled to a better life, the sooner you will get one. Your goal is to imagine yourself in a better life, with a lot more fun, gratification and rewards, a life without limitations and limitless possibilities.

Remember, the moment your imagination considers greater possibilities for you, you win. Once you know what is possible for you and you focus on what you want, you will begin to attract wonderful things into your life. The mind is a magnet and you can use it to draw into your life the things that you want the most. What you think about, you will bring about, so only focus on what you want. That's the key...**ONLY FOCUS ON WHAT YOU WANT.** You will be amazed and delighted with the opportunities to change and grow that will cross your path.

Finding your highest level of personal achievement begins in your imagination.

Here's what you can do...

Challenge yourself.

Control your thoughts.

Where you
look
is
where you
go!

LESSON 29

The Universe Always Accelerates a Plan

Have you ever noticed that once you set your mind on something, what you want seems to appear in your life as if by magic? Your willingness and ability to focus on what you want to change in your life can attract into your life all of your desires. The human mind is a powerful tool, a tool that you can use to your advantage. You literally have the ability to think about what you want, and as a result of that thought, plant a seed in your mind that can become your reality. What you think about comes about. And when you consider that we have about 45,000 to 50,000 thoughts a day, the more intensely you focus on what you want, the greater the likelihood that it will appear in your life. I am not referring to wishing, although wishing is nice. I am speaking about intensely focused mental energy directed toward what you want. Intensely focused mental energy is the key to changing your life; the more committed you are, the better your life will become, starting now.

How does this work? I am not exactly certain. However, I

have seen enough evidence to know that your mind has a miraculous ability to attract into your life the things that are most important to you. So how it works is not nearly as important as you believing that it does. You don't have to know exactly how a fax machine works in order to use one. Likewise, utilizing the power of your mind does not require that you understand how things happen, they will just happen. Not only can you create the opportunities to change your life by what you focus on, typically the things that will change in your life will change even faster than you expect.

Your faith, confidence and belief that the power of your mind can change your life are essential to change. Ultimately you will only get the things that you believe that you deserve, and the more confident you are about changing your life circumstances, the closer you become to having all that you desire. The belief that has worked best for me is the things that I want most, want me. Empowered with the belief that the things that you want most will eventually be part of your life is a tremendous way to approach your future. Beginning each day with an expectation that great things will happen to you and that you are changing for the better is a terrific way to go through life. And as long as you have the freedom to control the quality of your thoughts and as long as BIG THINKING IS FREE, you only benefit by entertaining these beliefs. In fact, the more you are willing to embrace this attitude and behavior, the more you change your life for the better.

Of course, in order for your plan to be accelerated, you must first have a plan. Unfortunately, most people approach each day without a plan or, at best, their plan is to make it through today and get to tomorrow. Regrettably, that just won't suffice. I'm speaking about a genuine road map that you can follow each day, with each day bringing you closer to your desired outcome. The key to creating your plan demands that you employ your future vision. Your ability to look beyond where you are right now and envision where you will be when your mental images become your reality requires focus and discipline. This type of thinking requires confidence, creativity, certainty, clarity and commitment. Because, the more certain you are about the end result of your plan, the more likely you will get what you want and when you get it, it will be faster than you expect. Your plan must be carefully conceived, paying great attention to all of the details, time frames and actions that you must take. The more physical and mental energy you invest in creating your plan, the better. The more specific your plan, the clearer it will be in your mind. Once your mind knows what you want, you are on your way to significant life change.

Once your plan is written, oh yes, **IT MUST BE IN WRITING,** keep reworking it until it accurately reflects exactly what you want. If you think that just knowing you want to change your life is enough, think again. Your commitment to putting your future on paper is powerful. My philosophy has always been, "If it's not in writing, it doesn't exist." So write down what you want, in priority order, the more specific the better, with timetables for accomplishment and necessary actions to be taken. Always remember the mind works in pictures; the more vivid you can make your plan, the more your limitless subconscious mind can bring your plan to reality. Remember, you do not need to know HOW it's going to happen, you just need to know what you want and maintain a positive attitude of expectation. One more thing about your plan, only share it with the people in your life who will support you in getting what you want. The more powerful your personal support system, the faster you will achieve change and the more you will stay committed to improving your life. You can change your destiny and change it faster than you expect or imagine. To do so, you need a written plan. Write one NOW!

What you want most, wants you. When you believe that you can change your life, you will…and fast!

Here's what you can do…

Write a limitless plan for your life.

Always imagine your plan working perfectly.

The cure for frustration is action...

LESSON 30

Life's Solution is About Execution

Having a detailed plan is just one of the keys to changing your life and getting what you want. Ultimately, transforming your life will come down to your ability to consistently execute the plan you have created. Carrying out your plan is the bottom line in making a better future for yourself. So while change has a lot to do with knowing exactly what you want, without a strong personal commitment to act on, you will only become disappointed and frustrated. All Masters of Change have a step-by-step strategy that they adhere to as they move closer to their desired outcome. Masters of Change stay focused on their outcome and make certain that whatever actions they take bring them closer to what they want.

Eventually, changing your life all comes down to your ability to execute your plan. Remember, you cannot change your life by doing the things that have created the life you presently have. Want change? Then you have to do something, something different from what you have always done. You can either wait for change to happen to you or you can make decisions and take actions that will determine the rest of your life. It's your choice.

In order for you to get the maximum change possible, you have to first identify what is possible for you. Once you know what's possible, then you need to become crystal clear about the pressures that will be exacted on you, as well as the risks that you will need to take and the resources that are available to you. When you are clear about what is necessary for you to do, you can willingly pay the price and do it. And, like all change, there is going to be a price to pay. One other thing, as you embark on the execution of your plan, be prepared to experience some failure along the way. Most of the things you have learned in life, you learned from trying and failing. Remember, when it comes to changing your life, it's okay if you fail, it's not okay if you quit. Then, keep moving in the direction of your dreams. Staying true to your action strategy in the face of failure is a demonstration of your level of personal commitment. So take some chances along the way and stick to your plan. Being a winner in life is a choice; winners always get up one more time than they are knocked down. Your goal is to continue to execute your plan until you reach your desired destination. You just keep moving forward. Why? Because you are committed to change, that's why.

It has been said that most of the frustrations we experience in life are the result of disappointments, either in others or ourselves. When you become frustrated, do something. Do anything, as long as what you do moves you closer to what you want. Take actions that are meaningful, actions that you believe bring you nearer to your outcome as opposed to actions just for actions' sake. Masters of Change understand that there is a big difference between being busy and being successful. So, do the constructive things that move you in the direction of the success you want.

Success, like change, is seldom linear. Rarely do people consistently change their lives in an upward direction without some setbacks along the way. And that's okay.

This is the important thing for you to remember, each day you may gain some new success and each day you may actually lose some old success. Your goal is to make certain that you gain a little more success each day than you lose. With that philosophy as your driving force, it becomes your responsibility to make sure that your plan of action brings you just a bit closer to what you want every single day. Do so, and ultimately you can have the life of your dreams.

So move forward in the direction of your dreams each and every day. No matter what, move forward. Regardless of what others say or think, move forward. When you feel tired, move forward. When you think you are stuck with the life you have, move forward. When all seems helpless, move forward. When you are faced with overwhelming odds, move forward. When you fail, move forward.

What you do does not cause stress. It's what you think about doing and fail to do that causes the stress in your life. Move forward.

Here's what you can do…

Do more than you ordinarily do.

Envision success as the end result of your actions.

All great achievement begins with a question.

LESSON 31

Work Backwards

So, what do you want? All great, permanent, significant and meaningful change begins with a question. "What do you want? What do you really want?" Search your mind and challenge your imagination and come up with a specific answer. Once you have that answer, you are on your way. A clear vision is the genius of all creativity and the clearer you are about your future, the more you will create opportunities that deliver the outcome you desire.

Unfortunately, most people go through life without a clear vision of what they really desire and, as a result, they never realize their aspirations. The depth of their daily thought process mostly surrounds either making it until tomorrow or, at best, merely knowing that they want a life filled with more things, better things or different things than what they currently have. This is clearly not the best way to improve your life.

Rather, I suggest a formula that has worked incredibly well for me in the past and continues to do so. Follow the formula and it will work well for you, but you must stick to the formula. This formula enters into all of my strategic planning and has been instrumental in improving the quality of my life. I work the formula whenever I am confronted with change or want to create change. As long as I adhere to the formula, I always seem to wind up better off, and you will too. Everyone should have a formula for change. If you don't have one as yet, I strongly suggest that you use mine. It will serve you well as long as you work the formula on a daily basis and work backwards. That means that the very first thing you have to know is precisely what you want. Then construct a specific series of actions that will deliver that end result. I call this reverse engineering your life. You should always begin with the end result in mind and then create a plan that supports you in attaining that outcome. Whenever you focus your physical and mental energy on outcomes, you will attract into your life all of the people and situations necessary for you to accomplish your goal.

My formula for change is: 3W+H=CHANGE.

Here is what 3W+H=CHANGE stands for. The first W in 3W stands for WHAT YOU WANT IN PRECISE TERMS. The second W stands for WHEN YOU ARE GOING TO HAVE IT BY. The third W is all about your WHY, your purpose, why you want what you want. Those are the 3 W's. The H is your HOW. How you are going to make your 3 W's a reality. That's it; my formula for maximizing your natural human potential and it all begins with you having a clear vision.

WHAT YOU WANT IN PRECISE TERMS—This is where you identify your outcome, the end result you are committed to creating and those changes that you want to occur. Your desired outcome must be in writing. You need to list exactly what you want, paying great attention to each and every detail. Because the mind works in specifics, not generalities, the more exact you are the better. Knowing precisely what you want is a critical step in changing your life. Without clarity of direction, I suppose that anywhere you wind up is probably good enough. This is not the time to settle for less than you believe you deserve. On the contrary, this is the time to make some bold, dramatic and specific life changing decisions.

WHEN ARE YOU GOING TO HAVE IT BY? Your WHEN is your timetable for the completion of your outcome. It's your own personal deadline. You have to approach it with tremendous creativity, resourcefulness and urgency. Everything that you think about and all that you do has to be deadline oriented. I strongly suggest that you keep your deadlines tight rather than distant. Distance tends to create resistance and the further out your deadlines, the more you will resist reaching them. The risk that most people face with distant deadlines is that they can lose interest along the way and nothing gets accomplished. I prefer to break deadlines into smaller attainable time frames. This is the way that you should approach each task. Breaking your deadlines into smaller deadline will help you stay focused and give you a positive feeling of achievement as you move forward. This technique helps me stay focused and gives me the feeling of accomplishment as I work toward my ultimate outcome. Try it. Regardless of how you select to handle your self-imposed deadlines, you must have a specific deadline and the discipline to NEVER move your completion date back. If you move your date, you make it too easy to move other dates in the future and the next thing you know, nothing ever gets completed. A deadline is a deadline!

WHY—is about your true underlying purpose. Your WHY is the reason that you want what you want. Your WHY is the thing that drives you toward change and achieving excellence. It is your inspiration, your personal passion, the reason that you get up each day. It's the source of your physical strength and mental resolve. People without a passionate purpose for change very often lose interest in their outcome and end up living a life filled with boredom and frustration. A crystal clear purpose will continually rekindle your spirit, keep you motivated, and enliven your will to accomplish great things.

Remember, your three W's must be specific in outcome, measurable in a set time frame, visually clear in your mental image and agreed upon where other people are concerned. Plan your life, don't just let it happen.

HOW—Your HOW is your POA (Plan of Action). Basically, you can have whatever you want, whenever you want it and for whatever reason you desire, as long as you have an action plan that supports your outcome. Masters of Change are massively action oriented. They recognize that the bottom line to all achievement is action, efficient, meaningful and focused action. So this is the time for you to become massively action oriented. And all of your actions must be directed to delivering the specific outcome that you want. Then, continue working in the direction of your dreams until you arrive at your desired destination. Masters of Change are tireless in their pursuit of excellence, and they work their plan with exactness and consistency. Once you have created your written plan of action, review it and make certain that it is capable of giving you the outcome that you want. If it is, work your plan. If it isn't, continue to rework your plan until you are confident that execution of your plan of action will get you the change that you are looking for. Your HOW must allow you to focus specifically on the attainment of your goal.

You can have whatever you want IF you know when you want it by, are clear about your purpose, and work your action plan to make it reality.

Here's what you can do…

Be deadline oriented.

Become a master of specificity.

Control
your focus
and
you control
your destiny.

LESSON 32

The Unpredictable Nature of Life

This next to last lesson was written as I sat in the surgical waiting room at LDS Hospital in Salt Lake City, Utah. I had been here since noon. It was after 6 P.M. and my wife Laura was still in surgery. Quite frankly, this was about the most challenging day of my life. The changes that occurred in our lives and the lives of our family over those few months had been fast, furious and dramatic. Things were just perfect weeks before, until Laura discovered a lump in her right breast. We had been married for almost 20 years, and Laura is not only the best person who I have ever met, she is my best friend in the world and had always been unshakable and indestructible.

Who ever thought that one little lump could change so many lives? The month prior to surgery had been filled with surgeons, biopsies, tests, evaluations, opinions and choices. All scary. Even more frightening was the fact that Laura has had normal mammograms for the past ten years. How could this have happened to us? Well, it did happen to us and the more I learned, the more I came to realize that the incidence of breast cancer in this country is staggering. In terms of change, this is about as big as it gets!

Amazing how the things that you thought were important yesterday can seem so unimportant today.

Amazing how one change can put everything in your life into perspective immediately.

Amazing how we tend to take all good things in our lives for granted.

Amazing how we waste time when, in fact, time is clearly the most precious resource we have.

Amazing how all the detailed plans that you have made for the rest of your life can be thrown into utter and complete turmoil.

Talk about change, something like this can change you, fast and forever. Life events can create change in a flash.

There is an unpredictable part of life that constantly challenges and surprises us. And, while we know that sometimes "stuff" can happen to anyone at anytime, we tend to believe that some things will never happen to us. You know, the kind of things we hear about and we believe that we are immune to. Things that happen to other people, not us. Well, they do happen to us, like it or not, and we are all exposed to the possibility of BIG change at any given time.

At 10 P.M., and after 6½ hours of surgery, Laura had just been brought up to her room from recovery. Nothing in my life had prepared me for how she looked or for the discomfort she was experiencing. Not to mention the sick and helpless feeling that I was experiencing. Yet, through it all, her strength, courage and beauty were evident. Clearly she was and still is the most extraordinary person I have ever known. People have always told me just how fortunate I was to be married to Laura, and they were right.

The next 36 hours proved to be filled with change, stress and anxiety. Watching Laura lie almost helpless was gut wrenching. The effects of the morphine and other pain killing drugs left her flat on her back, except for the occasional nausea and vomiting. Change can really hurt. Not just you, but those around you. Just as Laura was starting to return to herself, the surgeon stopped by to check her and give us the results of her pathology tests. The great news was that the cancer had not reached her lymph nodes. It's impossible to express the positive emotion that filled the room at that moment. It was the best we could hope for in a horrible situation. We were elated. The depression of the past few days was instantly replaced with hope and optimism. Oh, we knew we still had a big battle in front of us, but hope had replaced despair. That's how fast change can happen. Sometimes change can make life almost impossible, and sometimes change can make life more bearable. That's why mental and emotional flexibility is so important.

All life changes, regardless of size—even those changes that are excruciatingly painful—provide the opportunity for personal growth.

Our new challenge and adventure were just beginning. We knew that the next few years would be filled with anxiety, change, and sacrifice and would demand great personal courage.

So, for us and for you, the changes just keep right on coming. Change stops when you do.

I am confident that we are up to the challenges and changes that life will throw in our path, are you? You have enough information to change your life in any way that you desire. However, information is seldom enough to get the job done. The only thing that matters is what you do next. So what are you waiting for? Start changing.

You already have all that you need to meet any challenge.

Here's what you can do…

Be flexible.

Be grateful.

Change
takes
courage

LESSON 33

Change is the Only Certainty We Have

Who Knows What Adventures Lie In Store For Us?

Here's what you can do…

Use your time wisely.

Live your life to the fullest.

LESSONS LIST

Lesson 1 — All Change Is About Loss And Gain

…How you view change is up to you.

Lesson 2 — Everyone Wants More Or Less Of Something

…Changing for the better begins with a decision.

Lesson 3 — Change Perpetuates Change

…You can control the next change or the next change can control you…take charge.

Lesson 4 — There Is Always A Price To Pay

…Success is a NOW thing.

Lesson 5 — You're In The Pain...Or You're In The Pain

…The pain of change often leads to pleasure. Find the pain!

Lesson 6 — Decisions Determine Destiny

…Make some life changing decisions today AND stick to them.

Lesson 7 — Excuses Or Excellence

…Excellence is about your will, your attitude and your discipline. So, stop settling and go for excellence.

Lesson 8 — Change Your Behavior And You Change Your Life

...Your past behavior determined who you are...your future behavior determines who you become.

Lesson 9 — Change Is About Letting Go

...Let go of the known and pay the price of change.

Lesson 10 — Change Has Four Enemies

...Decide to conquer Fear, Amiability, Complacency and Ego.

Lesson 11 — Conquer Your Fears

...Every dream has a price and the price you may have to pay to live your dream is overcoming your fears. No more "What ifs."

Lesson 12 — Change Requires Accountability

...In an environment of zero accountability, it is difficult for most people to change permanently. Find a Change Coach.

Lesson 13 — It's Not What You Know...It's What You Do

...You change your life by advancing one step at a time.

Lesson 14 — Find Your Passion

...Find your passion and you find your stamina. Find your stamina and you can do anything.

Lesson 15 — Flexible Is Durable

...When it comes to change, flexible is durable...bend.

Lesson 16 — Complacency Kills Change

...The number one WAY to change...LIFE REWARDS ACTION, NOT COMPLACENCY. Why? Just BECAUSE.

Lesson 17 — You Get What You Expect

...Maintain an attitude of great expectations and you will get exactly what you expect.

Lesson 18 — Raise Your Standards

...Elevate your standards and you elevate the quality of your life.

Lesson 19 — Rapid Change Requires Rapid Response

...As long as you are going to change, change rapidly.

Lesson 20 — Catch F.I.R.E.

...Focus, Intensity, Resourcefulness and Enthusiasm are the keys to change.

Lesson 21 — The Price Of Change Comes In Many Forms

...Be willing to exchange the life you are living for the life you want to live.

Lesson 22 — You Learn When You Are Ready

...If you are serious about change, keep learning and thinking how to make each day a happy day.

Lesson 23 — Your Image Impacts Change

...Regardless of what you desire, your personal image must be larger than your vision.

Lesson 24 — Change Happens When You Do

...You change your life and make things happen by exploring what can be done newer, more, better and differently.

Lesson 25 — Live The 4 C's

...Character, courage, commitment and confrontation are the tools of change.

Lesson 26 — Manage Your Emotions

...Manage your emotions or your emotions manage you. It's your choice.

Lesson 27 — Make Money Your Slave

...You determine your financial destiny.

Lesson 28 — Find Out What's Possible

...Finding your highest level of personal achievement begins in your imagination.

Lesson 29 — The Universe Always Accelerates A Plan

...What you want most, wants you. When you believe you can change your life, you will...and fast!

About The Author

Danny Drubin has lived in a world of constant change for his entire life. Born and raised in New York City, Danny has survived all of the challenges of a ghetto childhood, a broken home and innumerable life challenges by becoming a Master of Change. He is a graduate of New York Chiropractic College and practiced Chiropractic for seventeen years on Long Island, New York. During Danny's life, he has shoveled snow and raked leaves for spending money, worked in a tailor shop, been a delivery boy at a pharmacy, worked as a busboy at a catering company, unloaded trucks on the night shift at a supermarket, ran a day camp, caddied, managed 2 clothing stores in Greenwich Village, NY, designed and sold men's clothing, owned a jeans store, owned an Italian restaurant, worked as a mortuary caretaker at the Queens County City Morgue and manufactured cans at the Continental Can Company in Maspeth, NY.

For the past 30 years Danny has traveled across the country in the capacity of a management consultant, sales and marketing trainer, teacher, lecturer, motivational speaker, author and life change expert.

Danny is available as a personal Change Coach to a limited number of FEARLESS people who are prepared to do whatever it takes to improve their lives. He also does teaching and motivational presentations to large and small groups of people who are committed to transforming their lives.

An avid skier and struggling golfer, Danny resides with his wife Laura and their children Peter and Jennifer in Park City, Utah.

Danny Drubin is indeed The Master of Change!